Bread Machine
Sweets and Treats

Bread Machine
Sweets and Treats

Featuring Tea Breads, Coffee Cakes, and Festive Desserts for All Occasions

Richard W. Langer

Illustrations by Susan McNeill

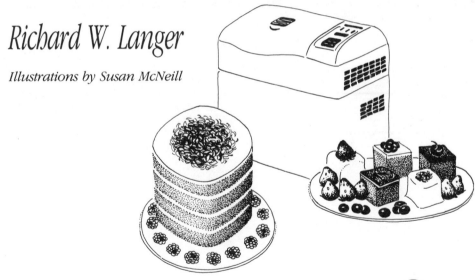

Little, Brown and Company

Boston   New York   Toronto   London

First Edition

Library of Congress Cataloging-in-Publication Data
Langer, Richard W.
  Bread machine sweets and treats : featuring tea breads, coffee cakes, and festive desserts for all occasions / Richard W. Langer ; illustrations by Susan McNeill. — 1st ed.
    p.   cm.
  Includes index.
  ISBN 0-316-51391-1
  1. Bread. 2. Automatic bread machines. 3. Desserts. I. Title.
TX769.L33   1993
641.8'15—dc20   93-16014

10 9 8 7 6 5 4 3 2 1

MV-NY

Published simultaneously in Canada by Little, Brown & Company (Canada) Limited

Printed in the United States of America

For Susan, who shared yet another one — at the computer, the art table, and the groaning board

Contents

1 · Hey, My Bread Machine Has a Sweet Tooth!

THANKS TO THE INTRODUCTION of automatic bread machines, the tantalizing fragrance of home-baked bread is probably filling more kitchens now than at any other time since the invention of sliced bread at the turn of the century. Bread machines reward their owners with all the pleasure and nourishment of homemade loaves in return for only minutes of preparation time and a minimum of bother.

"If only they could bake pastries as well!" is the echoing cry of today's busy gourmet. Well, they can.

Now, I'll be the first to admit that bread machines have their limitations when it comes to traditional cakes and quick breads. Their pans restrict the shape of the loaves they eject to a monotonous sameness, the crusts they produce are thicker than those of cakes and quick breads baked in conventional ovens in conventional cake or loaf pans, and they cannot accommodate pastries dependent on eggs and/or baking powder for their leavening (unless you use the machines as mere mixers, which then is not using them as bread makers). But there are ways around these problems, and finding them provided the impetus for this book. The recipes in it yield a broad range of sweets and treats you can make right in your bread machine.

Someday, probably soon, in fact, bread machines will become true home bakeries. It would take next to nothing for their manufacturers to reprogram the microchip controller directing all their actions to include a short baking-powder-bread cycle, for instance, or an initial egg-beating cycle for true cake batters.

It would also cost the manufacturers very little, if anything, to offer an assortment of pan shapes for the machines. At present, the round pans of DAK and Welbilt bread machines lend the sweets baked in them a more traditional cake shape than do the square pans of, say, the Hitachi or the Panasonic, while the oblong pan of the larger Panasonic yields a loaf looking more like the traditional loaf of bread. Why not simply offer buyers a selection of pan shapes as optional extras? After all, what cook has only one pie tin or cake pan?

Another convenience that could easily be added is a separate compartment, similar to the one for yeast featured on some machines, for ingredients that are best added to the dough at the last possible moment, like chocolate chips and nuts. True, there are machines that beep at you to indicate the proper time for such inclusions, but wouldn't it be nice if they simply went ahead and tossed them in as well?

Meanwhile, until the bread machine with all these accoutrements of the well-stocked bakery arrives on the market, I'll keep exploring ways around the limitations of the ones available. Being an inveterate experimenter, and liking cakes as much as I do bread, I've come up with a number of recipes adapted for bread machines that yield really delightful treats capable of satisfying just about anyone's sweet tooth. With little more effort than tossing the ingredients into the pan and pressing a button, you can coax from any of the bread machines currently on the market a wide range of sweets, from a fragrant, spicy kumquat tea loaf to a devilishly dense chocolate cake, and from the simplest *biscotti* to a spectacular *panettone farcito*.

It's true that different makes and models of bread machines yield somewhat different loaves, even when the same recipe is used for all of them. The Chocolate Nut Delight cake produced by a Hitachi using the recipe in this book, for instance, is somewhat larger and crustier than the one turned out by a National or a Panasonic, which is more open-textured and chewy. But both are scrumptious loaves.

Certain recipes, however, do not lend themselves to large-quantity measurements and large pans. The ingredients called for are too viscous or too unwieldy to be collected by the willing but small kneading blade from all the corners of an oblong pan like that of the Panasonic or the National 1½-pound-loaf model, for example. Or they may be too weighty to be kneaded by the blade of a machine like the Hitachi, whose pan, because it is so tall, can physically contain the ingredients for either a small or a large loaf but may not be able to mix the greater batch. Hence you'll find some recipes in the book designed only for the small, or 1-pound, loaf.

Where a recipe has worked well for both small and large loaves, I have included both — with one caveat. If you are using a machine with an oblong baking pan for a large loaf, lift the lid and peek inside at about 5 or 10 minutes into the preliminary mixing cycle to see how the dough is forming. A bread machine's kneading blade is designed to collect the ingredients placed in the baking pan around it until they form a ball, which then careens around the pan picking up any little leftover scraps of ingredients the blade didn't catch. So a dough too soft to form a ball may fail to pick up all the flour from the edges of the pan. If when you take your peek you find that the mixing blade hasn't collected all the ingredients into a tidy ball, scrape down the sides of the pan with a rubber spatula to help it along. Sneaking a look at the dough's progress is perfectly all right during the kneading cycle. Just don't open the lid on a machine that has a separate container for leavening built into it at about the time when the yeast is scheduled to be released into the dough, for obvious reasons. You also want to refrain from disturbing the environment of the miniature bakery later in the bread-making process, when the bread is rising. And I burned my nose once peeking during the baking cycle.

Certain sticky chocolate doughs and those of moist, milk-based cakes sometimes fail to form a smooth ball of dough even when the batch is a small one. A little extra flour will often firm up such a dough and improve the final results.

In a lightweight machine like the DAK or the Welbilt, a dense, substantial dough may also require a bit of outside help during mixing, this time in the form of an adjustment to the recipe. The kneading blades of the lightweights simply haven't the power to handle a heavy dough well. If your machine seems to be struggling to knead a particular dough, barely churning it in its pan, add a little extra liquid, a tablespoonful at a time. The telltale sign of an inadequately mixed dough is unevenly dispersed ingredients in the finished loaf. But by then it's too late to remedy the situation. Better to listen to what your machine is trying to tell you.

Very few other adjustments need to be made in the recipes in this book to accommodate individual machines. One that does come to mind is the timely incorporation of the yeast, which depends primarily on whether your machine has a separate yeast dispenser. You will need to consult the directions that came with your particular machine in deciding when the yeast should be added and in what order the other ingredients should be measured into your baking pan.

Another small adjustment concerns the addition of mush-able ingredients you don't want mushed. Machines with beepers that tell you when it's time to add such ingredients have the advantage here. Without such a signaling device, you'll need to rely on your watch or a timer to remind you to add the morsels. The alternative, of course, is simply to allow the ingredients to be mixed in with the others, which as often as not is quite satisfactory. The two exceptions I can think of here are chocolate chips and berries, fresh or dried.

Most loaves bake well in a bread machine set to its quick cycle (on some machines called the rapid-bake mode), which is shorter than the regular cycle by about an hour. Since the extended baking cycle for whole wheat breads available on the newer National and Panasonic machines is not an option on many of the others, I've rarely relied on it in perfecting a recipe for general bread machine use, although it does extend the rising time for a loaf. The same goes for the crisp-crust setting, which extends the leavening period even further — without, as far as I can see, any noticeable effect on the finished loaf.

By all means, experiment with the extended cycles if they are available on your machine, with the proviso that they may or may not make a difference. For while all bread machines work, they do have their own small idiosyncrasies, just as a regular oven does.

The light, medium, and dark settings for loaf color found on many machines are a matter of individual choice. With rare exceptions, such as fig and date cakes or other naturally dark loaves, I use the default setting the machine itself selects automatically when turned on. The device is programmed by the manufacturer to use that setting, unless instructed to move to another, because that's the one most often used.

Daily temperature fluctuations, atmospheric conditions, altitude, flour quality — flours differ not only from brand to brand but even from harvest to harvest — and even the size of an egg can all affect the final product of a certain recipe. A loaf that emerges from your electronic oven with a swirly pattern on top or a tipsy topknot is telling you that your particular machine had a problem mixing that particular batter. Well, there's nothing wrong with a swirly top as long as the loaf beneath is satisfactory. But it might bear watching next time around.

A dense loaf, especially, may need a little help exiting from its pan, since it will tend to cling to the beater in the bottom of the pan. Rapping the pan on the edge of the counter sometimes helps. So does turning the screw on the underside of the pan back and forth a few times. Remember to use a pot holder when you try that one.

On the whole, however, you should find that your bread machine can turn out all on its own a bounty of consistently good loaves needing just a touch of kitchen artistry to turn them into delightful sweets. While a loaf is cooling, you'll have time to make a sauce for it, shave some chocolate to sprinkle over it, or whip up a quick icing. None of the treats included in this volume should take more than 10 or 15 minutes to assemble, and many are quickies that take only a minute or two. "Oh, how sweet it is," as Jackie Gleason used to say.

2 · Caramel Cream, Cocoa Dust, and Other Sweet Touches

 BREADS AND CAKES are basically the same fare. What separates the one from the other is more a matter of expectations than anything else. This is not to say that a slice of rye bread becomes, on being covered with chocolate icing, a cake. Exactly what it does become I'm not sure; that it exists I have no doubt. Our children have been known to slather Nutella, that delightful chocolate-hazelnut spread from Italy now seen in many stores in this country, on any bread that's handy.

When I came to this country as an immigrant in the late forties, bread was still central to my life. Even in Sweden, neutral during the war and undamaged physically, the economic consequences of that worldwide confrontation were great, and so we ate a lot of bread. Very good bread.

Most of the bread I found in this country was a puffy white tasteless disaster compared with the solid peasant loaves to which I was accustomed. The ice cream, however, was fantastic, a boy's dream come true. It could make up for just about anything.

One day about six months after we had reached these shores, I was in a local candy store learning English, of which I had known not a word before arriving in the States, by reading *Fox and the Crow* and other comic books. A boy about my age entered, swaggered up to the soda fountain, and asked for an ice cream sandwich.

An ice cream sandwich! I had never heard of such a marvelous thing. Here were my two favorite foods combined. I too swaggered up to the counter and, in my best English, requested "one ice cream sandwich, please, on rye."

Besides expectations, appearance has much to do with what is considered a cake and what is not. The classic European tortes, such as the Sacher torte of Vienna, are not really sweet at all by modern cake-mix standards. It is their opulent fillings and frostings that make them so — which brings us to the bread machine as cake machine.

The fluffy cake as we know it relies on eggs, and often baking powder, to give it loft and lightness. It also happens to incorporate a fair amount of sugar. A bread machine, however, does not easily handle quantities of any of those ingredients. Eggs it cannot beat; baking powder it renders helpless by long sitting; large amounts of sugar kill the yeast it must rely on for leavening power. In short, to use contemporary jargon, bread machines don't do cakes, at least as we usually think of them.

On the other hand, they do turn out very rich loaves when called upon to do so. And a very rich loaf with a rich filling or frosting is fit for display in any *pâtisserie* window. Certainly it is fit to be served on your prettiest cake plate. One doesn't even miss the reduced calories in the layers themselves. Maybe, in fact, for some that's an added advantage of bread machine cakery.

Of course, a bread machine loaf fresh from the electronic oven is also delicious unadorned, simply sliced and served with perhaps a fruit spread or sweet butter. The choice is yours, then — plain or fancy, designer dessert or down-home fare. In either case, the loaf whose finished look you're contemplating is apt to be a pretty nutritional one as pastries go.

Many of the loaves whose recipes are found in this book are very healthy fare indeed. A number of them incorporate dried fruits and nuts, full of vitamins and minerals, and ingredients such as the millet and semolina flours used in many of them offer much more nourishment than cake flour does.

A white whole wheat flour newly developed at Kansas State University of Agriculture and Applied Science that has all the vitamins, minerals, and fiber of the whole wheat kernel without the faint bitter aftertaste of whole wheat promises to become an excellent substitute for white flour. While it appeared on the market too late for me to test it with a variety of loaves, you'll find it in the Zwieback and Cherry Milk Loaf recipes in this book, where I put it to use with great success. This flour will likely replace all-purpose flour in a good many of my future recipes.

But for now the basic so-called white flour in my personal bread machine bakery is the unbleached variety, whitened naturally by aging. I much prefer it to bleached flour, which is whitened through chlorination. However, bleached flour can be substituted for unbleached in any of the recipes in this book calling for all-purpose flour, as can the newer bread flour, a flour with a higher gluten content than ordinary flour. I've simply found it an unnecessary addition to the larder, since regular flour works perfectly well.

You may be surprised to find no cake flour in any of the recipes in this volume. Cake flour would seem the flour best suited of all to delicate, sweet loaves, because it's lighter than ordinary flour. And indeed it is suited to true cakes, which rely on eggs or baking powder rather than yeast for their leavening power. But, as it happens, cake flour also contains less gluten than all-purpose flour, and gluten is what allows bread dough to expand as it is leavened by the yeast. So cake flour, contributing less of that elastic, airy quality, results in a smaller, denser yeast bread.

Millet and semolina flours are well suited to sweet treats from the bread machine bakery. The millet adds a light, moist crunchiness to a loaf, while semolina lends it silkiness and a warm, golden color. Millet, a staple of the human race for millennia, was at one point more popular than rice in China, and it is still a major food crop in Africa. Semolina, milled from protein-rich durum wheat with only the bran layer removed, is a traditional pasta flour favored for its high gluten content.

Other flours such as barley and oats will also be found among the ingredients in this book. Like semolina, barley gives a loaf a nutlike sweetness and a fine crumb. Oats, one of the grains richest in protein and minerals, add both texture and flavor, especially when used in their least-processed form. Cornmeal and bran do the same, each in its own distinctive fashion.

The whole-grain flours, because they contain perishable oils from the germ, or heart, of the grain, are best kept refrigerated. For long-term storage, they can also be frozen in airtight containers. It's handy to tuck them away in small plastic freezer bags in recipe-size portions.

Speaking of recipe portions, you may wonder why I do not specify sifting the flour or particularly the confectioners' sugar used for any of the sweets described in this book. Well, it seemed to me that since the whole principle of using a bread machine is supposed to be its convenience, it would be more useful to the reader and baker for me to adjust the amount of any given ingredient so the flour sifter would not have to be hauled out. Certainly any clumping of such ingredients as sugar is taken care of by either the kneading blade of the bread machine, if it's responsible for the mixing, or the beaters of the electric mixer, if that's what's doing the blending.

Convenience does need to give way to a little advance planning occasionally. For example, freezer-stored ingredients require a little warm-up time before use. Chunky ingredients frozen to retain their freshness, such as nuts and dried fruits, need half an hour's defrosting time. The exception that proves the rule is chocolate chips, which I suggest keeping in the freezer for certain sweets precisely so they will keep their separate identity when added to a dough.

In traditional culinary practice, all the ingredients for baking are brought to room temperature before being used. But while I wouldn't use flour straight from the freezer for a recipe, I don't hesitate to take items from the refrigerator as needed and add them straightaway to the baking pan. Merely chilly ingredients my bread machine can deal with. By the time they've gone through the initial kneading cycle, they're quite warm enough. Here the exception is a large quantity of butter. When a recipe calls for ¼ cup or more of butter, I cut it into smaller pieces before adding it to the dough, for otherwise it fails to be distributed evenly.

One of the bakery staples I keep in the refrigerator is my yeast, since, experimenting with as many loaves as I do, I buy it in bulk and thus usually have a sizable quantity on hand. Because the only brand of yeast I've come across that's purchasable in bulk is Red Star, that's the brand I happen to use, and I've found it highly satisfactory. But there are certainly other brands that work well, and the choice is largely a matter of personal preference derived from experience. I have experimented with the rapid-rise variety on the market, but that one I've found unpredictable when used in a bread machine.

Yeast converts the carbohydrates in a bread dough to carbon dioxide gas, which is what expands the dough, giving the finished loaf its light, airy texture. These carbohydrates — from white sugar to brown and from corn syrup to molasses — also contribute much of a loaf's flavor. In a bread dough, however, they cannot be used in overly large quantities, because the yeast is easily smothered by sugars. This is why the recipes in this book will produce lovely loaves, and often very rich-tasting ones, but never the ultrasweet ones associated in many people's minds with true cakes. You'll find the chocolate loaves, particularly, sumptuous but unsweet, so don't expect brownies from a bread machine. Do expect a surprising richness and intense flavor.

In case you're wondering about sugar substitutes, they don't work in the bread machine bakery. Most of them lose their sweetness in the prolonged high temperatures of the oven, leaving a bitter aftertaste in the baked loaf.

The various natural sweeteners usually can be substituted one for another. In substituting a granular sugar for a syrupy one, however, you may need to increase the amount of liquid called for in the recipe.

The liquid used in a cake recipe is almost always a dairy one. Water makes for a crisp crust, often desirable on a bread, seldom on a cake. Generally speaking, the richer the liquid, the more tender the loaf and softer the crust will be. Thus many of the recipes in this book call for cream, either sweet or sour, or buttermilk or yogurt.

Butter, for which canola and other light oils often can be substituted, also adds tenderness to a loaf. The butter I use is the unsalted variety, simply because that's what's at hand in our household, but salted butter is fine so long as you adjust the amount of salt you use accordingly. As for substituting an oil for the butter in a recipe, where either is fine, I have listed both — for example, "1 tablespoon unsalted butter or canola oil." Where I have felt that butter is strongly preferred, I have indicated the substitute in parentheses. Where only butter will do, no alternative is presented.

One normally doesn't think of salt in connection with sweets. Many cake recipes don't call for it. However, what we're working with here is yeast-based loaves, and the fact is that a little salt in the dough regulates and stabilizes the activity of the yeast.

Eggs are a supplementary leavening agent. They help to make a loaf wonderfully light. But the dozen eggs called for in a conventionally made torte, say, won't be found in the recipes for bread machine sweets — which, I might add, is all to the good for those watching their cholesterol consumption. The eggs for a cake, whole or separated, are whipped to a froth, something a bread machine can't do. The purpose served by all that whipping, which is to incorporate air into the batter, is here served primarily by the yeast and kneading.

Almost all the ingredients for the recipes in this book can be found at the supermarket or at a health-food store. For any more exotic items not stocked locally, and for mail-order purchases, baking suppliers are listed at the back of the book, in the section "Sources for Baking Ingredients."

Browsing for ingredients, both in different stores and among the pages of mail-order bakery catalogs, often affords inspiration for new treats to coax from the bread machine. That's how I discovered the dried bananas that suggested the fabulous Banana Chocolate Loaf. It's also how macadamia nuts precipitated the Luau Loaf.

All manner of nuts and dried fruits make their appearance in these recipes. I've become quite partial to the dried fruits, from the familiar dates and prunes to blueberries and cherries — yuppie raisins, our daughter Tanya calls them. They are preferable to fresh ones in bread machine baking for a number of reasons.

For one thing, dried fruits tend to hold together more during the machine's heavy kneading process, resulting in chunks of contrast in the finished loaf rather than a homogeneous texture. For another thing, the intense, concentrated essence of the dried fruits adds much more flavor than their fresh or canned counterparts do. The moisture in undried fruit limits the amount of it that you can use.

Because the dried fruits are so concentrated — it takes anywhere from six to ten pounds of fresh fruit to produce a pound of dried — these wonderful tidbits are expensive. But they are well worth the price for their flavor and ease of use, not to mention nutrition. Stored in an airtight container, they keep almost indefinitely, which is another advantage they have over fresh fruit. They're available at a moment's notice.

From a tea loaf flecked with festive bits of dried cranberries or blueberries to a loaf adorned with a Satin Chocolate Glaze or a luscious caramel cream sauce is a very short step. And once that step is taken, what you'll find is that a cake has happened. Frostings, glazes, ice cream, toppings, nuts, and fruits all make opulent desserts out of simple loaves.

Commercial icings and syrups can be used to embellish most of the treats in this volume. However, I've also included recipes for homemade versions of the buttercreams, sauces, and other accompaniments that have seemed to go best with the different loaves I've baked. All of these additions are quickly made and applied, to match the quick-and-easy focus of bread machine baking.

Take that simple standby of the traditional kitchen, confectioners'-sugar icing. It's a no-fail crown for a cake that can be varied in a myriad of ways, for example, by substituting a liquid such as fruit juice, maple syrup, or hot fudge sauce for the plain water usually called for. If you add too much liquid by mistake, you can remedy it by simply adding more sugar. If it becomes too stiff, you can just dilute it with more liquid. It's almost impossible to botch.

A confectioners'-sugar icing lends itself to many different applications. Swirl it over a high-domed loaf or cut the entire loaf, except for the crusts, into squares an inch or two across and make petits fours of them. Trimming away the crusts, which leaves the remainder of a loaf much more cakelike, might at first seem rather wasteful. But there are great dessert uses for them, from homey bread puddings to wickedly rich fondues.

Petits fours look difficult to create, but they're really not, although it's true that they used to be. The classic fondant icing for petits fours is classically time-consuming to make, necessitating long cooking of the sugar syrup, cooling on a marble slab, and much folding and kneading — not exactly bread machine convenience.

Then too, the traditional method of frosting petits fours is something of a bother. First they are placed on a rack set in turn on waxed paper or a marble countertop and then coated with dribbled icing. Any fondant dripping off the pastries is then scraped up and reused. We're talking a glorious mess here.

But the cubes can be iced by simple dipping. Have a rack set on waxed paper or a cookie sheet ready to receive them once they're iced. Spear a cube with a fork and dip it into the saucepan holding the icing until all the sides except the bottom are coated, then lift it out and hold it above the saucepan for a moment to let most of the excess coating drip back into the pan. Now point it as right side up as you can over the rack and, using a second fork to help it along, slide the iced petit four off the first fork onto the rack. A little extra icing will still drip through onto the waxed paper or cookie sheet, but not a great deal.

Petits fours are prettily garnished with a strawberry — perhaps partly quartered, as one might cut a radish to reveal its white interior, and opened enough to hold a dollop of whipped cream or hard

sauce — or with kiwifruit circles or a kumquat sliced almost but not quite all the way through from top to stem and spread out to form a fan.

A single chocolate curl makes a striking statement on a white iced petit four. Curls are easily scraped from a square of semisweet chocolate with a vegetable parer if the chocolate is first warmed for a minute or two in the palm of your hand. For a nice accent on a colored icing, a chunk of fresh coconut can be pared in a similar fashion to form lacy white curls. Handle gently, for they will not only look, but be, very delicate. That's the beauty of them.

Another attractive white decoration is rosettes made from hard sauce piped through a pastry bag or a cookie press fitted with a star tip. If you pipe the rosettes out onto a foil-lined cookie sheet or tray and place them uncovered in the freezer, once hardened they can be transferred to a rigid container and kept frozen for up to six months, ready for use whenever a festive accent is needed.

Besides being cut into petit four squares, a dessert loaf can be served simply in slices spread with a soft buttercream icing. Like the rosettes, any extra buttercream left over can be frozen for later use. When it's needed, merely defrost it and whip it up again with an electric mixer for a couple of minutes until it is fluffy once more.

A soft icing can be scooped onto slices of a dessert loaf and swirled into a pretty pattern, or it can be spread over the slices and smoothed to a sheen with a spatula. A serrated knife run over it will create waves or ripples, depending on whether you draw the knife straight across the icing or zigzag it as you go.

For a contrasting motif on a buttercream icing, lay a paper doily over it, dip a small, soft brush like those used in watercolor (but not one that's been so used) into some cocoa, and tap it lightly over the doily with your forefinger. Remove the doily and you'll have an attractive stenciled pattern decorating the slice. If the buttercream is a chocolate or a mocha one, stencil it with confectioners' sugar instead of cocoa.

Another decorative touch for a frosted loaf is a piped design. Piping icings now come in handy toothpastelike tubes complete with a

variety of screw-on pattern tips. A striking design can be created by piping circles or lines of a trimming frosting onto the cake and then modifying its outlines by drawing a toothpick through the bands or stripes.

A square of semisweet chocolate microwaved in a plastic bag adaptable to that use makes a simple homemade decorating icing. Cut off a tiny corner of the bag, press the chocolate into that corner, and squeeze the bag gently. The chocolate will flow in a slender ribbon wherever you direct it.

Fruit is an age-old adornment for sweets. Sliced strawberries or grapes can be patterned to form a rose or a rosette covering the entire top of a cake. Peach or pear slices, fresh or canned, lend themselves to spiral and herringbone motifs. Pineapples make sunny daisies, especially if centered with a chocolate-dipped cherry. And, of course, orange and lemon slices can be slit and coiled into shapely curves, while their zest can be julienned and scattered in curls wherever you'd like a bright accent.

For added sparkle, canned fruits can be glazed with the syrup in which they were packed, reduced by about two thirds by boiling. Fresh fruits can be similarly glazed with apricot preserves or apple jelly brought to the simmering point. Dip the fruit in the glazing mixture, or drop it in and then remove it with a slotted spoon, and allow it to set for a few minutes before transferring it to your cake.

Nuts, chopped or whole, are another wonderful garnish for your bread machine bakery sweets. Almonds, particularly, lend themselves to being arranged in attractive patterns, from a pineapple of overlaid sliced blanched ones anchored in whipped cream to richly hued toasted ones garnishing some fabulous chocolate confection in a carefree scatter pattern. To brown almonds, bake them on a cookie sheet in a 350-degree F. oven or, for quicker results, crisp them in a dry skillet over medium heat, stirring to toast them evenly.

For whipped cream toppings, if the only cream you can find is the ultrapasteurized variety, that bane of the culinary arts, make sure it is very cold before trying to beat it. I've been known to put it in the freezer compartment of the refrigerator for a few minutes before attempting that endeavor, along with the bowl and beaters.

In the process of turning your bread machine loaves from plain to fancy treats, you'll acquire some leftovers. Not to worry. From simple brown Betty to elegant fondue, the crusts and crumbs from your baking, frozen for safekeeping till needed, will be put to excellent use.

Both a bread pudding and a fondue want a crusty, slightly stale bread. So it's an advantage to have on hand the trimmings from loaves used for other treats. Then too, the variety of loaves the different recipes in this book yield makes a basic fondue or bread pudding capable of almost infinite variety as well.

Even the crumbs from your loaves won't go to waste. They can be used to make delicious piecrusts of every flavor to fill with mousses and creams and summer fruit — quick, delightful desserts that the original designers of bread machines probably never dreamed of, and all of them tantalizingly different.

The simple truth is that when it comes to sweets and treats, the visual temptation is almost as important as the taste. What follows is a way to get both flavor and looks from your bread machine.

3 · Loaves for Tea and High Tea

HIGH TEA, THE AMERICAN VERSION of which traditionally featured coffee as the beverage of choice, is making a comeback. Granted, we're not talking about a massive social movement here. Nevertheless, more and more people are gathering as a family or with friends, on weekends or holidays at least, for coffee or tea and something special.

In the growing number of country inns dotting this land, teatime has become such an event that guests often plan their arrival to coincide with the occasion. According to the Professional Association of Innkeepers International, some 30 percent of member inns now serve afternoon tea. For some, tea has replaced the cocktail hour. Originally a ceremony for the British upper classes in need of an event to fill the long afternoons, teatime today is a respite from too few hours in which to do too much — a luxury of time, rest, and renewal.

The bread machine helps to give you time for tea when you don't have a butler and staff to provide it for you. The treats described on these pages can be served straight from the electronic oven with a simple accompaniment of sweet butter or a spread or fruit compote. For a company tea, take 10 minutes to make a fanciful pinwheel of a loaf fresh from your electronic oven sandwiched with the spread or compote and serve it on your prettiest cake platter. It will be an eye-catcher whose taste delights as well.

Apple Wheat Loaf

W e put a couple of big baskets filled with apples on the bay windowsill in our bedroom every fall. For sleeping, I like a cold bedroom (and a warm goose down comforter), so the apples keep well into December. The whole room is redolent with their fragrance, which my wife, Susan, likes as much as I do. She doesn't necessarily feel the same way about the nighttime temperatures in our sleeping quarters.

The time comes, however, when all the winter storage apples are gone — eaten out of hand or sliced into pies, the culls devoured to the last seed by the hens. Then we forage for the dried variety at the supermarket. Dried apples add a refreshing burst of flavor as well as nutrition to a winter loaf. The aroma of this one as it's baking is superb.

SMALL	LARGE
¾ cup buttermilk	*1¼ cups buttermilk*
2 tablespoons unsalted butter or canola oil	*3 tablespoons unsalted butter or canola oil*
2 tablespoons unsulfured molasses	*3 tablespoons unsulfured molasses*
¼ teaspoon lemon extract	*½ teaspoon lemon extract*
1 cup dried apples, packed	*1½ cups dried apples, packed*
1¼ cups unbleached all-purpose flour	*1¾ cups unbleached all-purpose flour*
1 cup whole wheat flour	*1¼ cups whole wheat flour*
1 teaspoon ground cinnamon	*1½ teaspoons ground cinnamon*
½ to 1 teaspoon salt, to taste	*1 to 1½ teaspoons salt, to taste*
1½ teaspoons active dry yeast	*2 teaspoons active dry yeast*

Pour the buttermilk into your bread machine baking pan and add the butter or canola oil, molasses, and lemon extract, unless the instructions that came with your machine specify that the yeast is to be placed in the bottom of the pan first thing, in which case these liquid ingredients should be added after the dry ones. Toss the dried apples into the pan, then measure in the all-purpose and whole wheat flours. Add the cinnamon, salt, and yeast, spooning the leavening into its own dispenser if a separate container is provided for it on your machine.

Use your machine's rapid-bake setting for this loaf.

Serve slices of the bread warm from the electronic oven with sweet butter, honey, or maple butter.

Light Citrus Loaf

The lightness of this loaf refers to its flavor, not to its substance. A diet cake it's not. But considering the millet and graham flours it incorporates, it's certainly not empty calories either.

The flavor and texture of the loaf are just right for creating a pinwheel cake, a lovely way to add sparkle to a late afternoon tea. The confection looks as if it took forever to make, when really it's quite simple and quick to construct.

In making a pinwheel, choose a filling for the striped vanes that will not add too much sweetness, since the tiny layers will use quite a bit of it. The rich colors of natural fruit preserves such as raspberry or blackberry add a stunning contrast. The lighter tones of apricot and peach lend the cake a quieter accent.

SMALL
3/4 cup buttermilk
1/4 cup sour cream or yohurt, regular or low-fat
2 tablespoons canola or other light oil
1 teaspoon lemon extract
1 teaspoon orange extract

LARGE
7/8 cup buttermilk
1/3 cup sour cream or yogurt, regular or low-fat
2 tablespoons canola or other light oil
1 1/2 teaspoons lemon extract
1 1/2 teaspoons orange extract

1 teaspoon vanilla extract	1½ teaspoons vanilla extract
1¾ cups unbleached all-purpose flour	2½ cups unbleached all-purpose flour
⅓ cup millet flour	½ cup millet flour
¼ cup graham cracker crumbs	½ cup graham cracker crumbs
¼ cup sugar	⅓ cup sugar
¼ to 1 teaspoon salt, to taste	½ to 1½ teaspoons salt, to taste
2 teaspoons active dry yeast	2½ teaspoons active dry yeast

If the instructions for your machine specify that the leavening is to be placed in the bottom of your baking pan first thing, add the dry ingredients next, the liquids last. Otherwise, place the buttermilk and sour cream or yogurt in the pan, followed by the oil and the lemon, orange, and vanilla extracts. Measure in the all-purpose and millet flours and add the graham cracker crumbs, sugar, salt, and yeast. If your machine features a separate dispenser for leavening, spoon the yeast in there; otherwise, scatter it over the rest of the dry ingredients.

Bake the loaf on the machine's quick cycle.

To make a pinwheel cake, once the cake has cooled, cut away the crusts to form an oblong. Laying the loaf on one of its long sides, slice it very thin. The bread accommodates slices no more than ¼ inch across if carved gently with a sharp serrated knife.

Next, starting at one end, spread a slice of the bread with fruit preserves, bringing the filling well out to the edges. Spread the next slice and lay it over the first. Continue to the end of the loaf, finishing with a plain slice. If the filling is overflowing the edges of the bread, run a knife around the edge of the stack to even up the sides. Then cut the reassembled loaf in thirds from top to bottom.

Keeping the slices firmly in place, turn the loaf on its side again and cut it diagonally from corner to corner. Eyeing the result of your labors, you'll find that what you've created is six fat striped triangles. Now you're ready to put the pinwheel together.

Place the triangles on a round serving platter, all facing the same way, so that they meet in the center. Ideally, their stripes will form

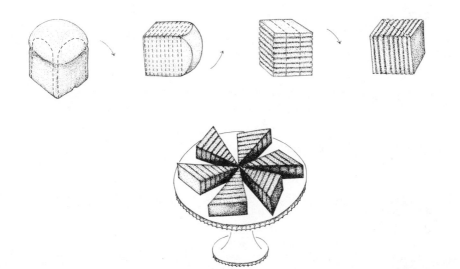

a spiral pattern. If any of them doesn't, simply flip the offending triangle over. A swirl of whipped cream or a circle of fruit added to the middle of the pinwheel is the nicest finishing touch for it.

A round loaf from a machine such as the Welbilt will produce striped semicircles instead of triangles. But it makes a lovely pinwheel all the same. It will need to have its first, thin slices run the length of the cylinder instead of across it. The second slicing, cutting it into thirds, should be crosswise. The final cut, instead of being on the diagonal (hard to find on a circle), should be at right angles to the stripes. The pinwheel blades will truly have the effect of running in circles.

Cherries and Cheese Loaf

Cheese makes its appearance in all types of baked goods, from the cream cheese found enriching a really solid New York–style cheesecake to the pot cheese adorning a Danish. Here, ricotta is put to good use with dried cherries.

A word about dried cherries. They're expensive, but they're worth it. Dried cherries add something special to a bread, and when you consider that it takes eight pounds or so of the fresh fruit to make a pound of the dried — in our family it would probably take sixteen, since no one would be just pitting the cherries when readying them for the drying rack — the price doesn't seem all that high. The nutritional value, on the other hand, does, for the wizened cherries are fairly packed with vitamins.

I particularly like the dried Montmorency cherries from Washington State for baking. Tart, tangy, and bursting with flavor, they also sparkle like liquid rubies in a snowy-white bread. Even when simply added with the other ingredients at the outset of operations, dried cherries, unlike raisins, are firm enough to survive your bread machine's kneading relatively intact. For the largest possible splashes of color, however, wait to add them until the machine beeps for add-ins, if it performs such oratory, or until the first kneading cycle is completed.

SMALL	LARGE
¼ cup water	⅓ cup water
¼ cup unsalted butter (or canola oil)	⅓ cup unsalted butter (or canola oil)
2 medium eggs	2 medium eggs
½ cup ricotta cheese	¾ cup ricotta cheese
½ teaspoon vanilla extract	1 teaspoon vanilla extract
2¼ cups unbleached all-purpose flour	3 cups unbleached all-purpose flour
2 tablespoons sugar	3 tablespoons sugar
	½ to 1½ teaspoons salt, to taste

¼ to 1 teaspoon salt, to taste
1½ teaspoons active dry yeast
⅓ cup dried cherries

2 teaspoons active dry yeast
½ cup dried cherries

Pour the water into your bread machine baking pan and add the butter (or canola oil). If you are using butter cold from the refrigerator, cut it into chunks before adding it to the pan, since otherwise it will not be incorporated uniformly into the other ingredients. Break the eggs into the pan and measure in the ricotta cheese, vanilla extract, flour, sugar, salt, and yeast, spooning the leavening into its own dispenser if your machine has one. However, should the directions for your machine specify that the yeast is to be placed in the bottom of the pan first thing, you'll need to remember to reverse the order in which you add the liquid and the dry ingredients.

Set the machine to its quick cycle for this bread and add the cherries at the beep or after the first kneading.

When the bread is served piping hot from its pan, the cherries are still moist inside, reminding one of a fresh cherry pie. Slices are delectable spread with cream cheese, and if you're one of those who can't stay away from the cherry jar, you can always sneak some more of them into the cream cheese too.

Pepparkaka (Swedish Spice Cake)

The most popular cake in the Sweden of my childhood was *sockerkaka,* a sponge cake whose name translates literally as "sugar cake." A more fragrant version of the cake, and my own favorite, was *pepparkaka,* or "ginger cake." Both used baking powder for their leavening, along with a quantity of eggs, but since a bread machine simply can't whip eggs to the proper froth, I substituted yeast in adapting an old family recipe for the machine — with notable success.

For the plainer *sockerkaka* omit the spices listed in the recipe and substitute either the grated zest of a lemon or a teaspoonful of vanilla extract, whichever your preference in flavors dictates.

Revell, the youngest of our children, likes his spice cake toasted and sprinkled liberally with cinnamon sugar. The rest of the family considers this practice wretched excess.

SMALL

1¼ cups milk, whole or skim
¼ cup unsalted butter (or canola oil)
1 medium egg
2 cups semolina flour
1½ cups unbleached all-purpose flour
⅔ cup sugar
1 teaspoon each ground ginger, ground nutmeg, ground cloves, and ground cinnamon (or 1 teaspoon vanilla extract or grated zest of 1 small lemon)
¼ to 1 teaspoon salt, to taste
1½ teaspoons active dry yeast

LARGE

1½ cups milk, whole or skim
⅓ cup unsalted butter (or canola oil)
1 medium egg
3 cups semolina flour
1¼ cups unbleached all-purpose flour
½ cup sugar
1½ teaspoons each ground ginger, ground nutmeg, ground cloves, and ground cinnamon (or 1½ teaspoons vanilla extract or grated zest of 1 large or 2 small lemons)
½ to 1½ teaspoons salt, to taste
2 teaspoons active dry yeast

Pour the milk into your baking pan and add the butter (or canola oil), unless the directions for your machine instruct you to start with the yeast, followed by the dry and then the liquid ingredients. If you are using butter straight from the refrigerator, cut it into chunks before placing it in the pan, so it will blend more easily with the other ingredients. Break the egg into the pan and add the semolina and all-purpose flours and the sugar. Add the ginger, nutmeg, cloves, cinnamon, and salt. For a plain sugar cake, substitute the vanilla extract or lemon zest for the spices and use a modest measure of salt. Spoon the yeast into its own dispenser if your machine has a separate container for leavening; otherwise, scatter it over the rest of the ingredients.

Use the machine's rapid-bake cycle for this loaf.

The aroma of a spice loaf permeates the house when it's baking, as you might have guessed from the ingredients. Serve it warm from its oven, when it's at its fragrant best. In Sweden, *pepparkaka* is a traditional accompaniment to strong black coffee for the grown-ups and *saft*, a delicately flavored fruit drink made from any number of natural fruit syrups diluted with water, for the children.

Panettone

Sophisticated Italian cooking, in a variety sending into near-oblivion mere spaghetti with meatballs and tomato sauce, has grown tremendously in popularity over the past decade. To my delight, this has brought osso buco and a number of other favorite dishes of mine to restaurant tables. But I've yet to become enamored of Italian desserts. The right one for me just hasn't come along. Like many non-Italians, I find Italian desserts to be this cuisine's weakest suit. Maybe it has something to do with being a noodle- and rice-based culture. The Chinese aren't exactly renowned for their desserts either.

Still, as the entrée menu has expanded far beyond pizza and pasta bolognese, so spumoni has been superseded by *tiramisù* and other exotic sweets.

There are two Italian desserts newly popular in this country that are well served by the bread machine's talents: *panettone* and the less well known *zuccotto,* a Florentine cream-filled cake.

Panettone is particularly well suited to bread machines having a round baking pan, since the loaf's traditional shape is like a chef's hat, cylindrical and tall. But certainly a square *panettone,* while perhaps disconcerting at first to those accustomed to its more conventional manifestation, is in no wise less tasty because of its figure.

The Christmas season in Italy would be unthinkable without the consumption of countless pieces of this cross between a cake and a sweet yeast bread. From the breakfast slice served with cappuccino or *caffellatte* to the delicate portion proffered with a glass of marsala or other sweet wine after dinner to the elaborate *panettone farcito* that is probably its most impressive rendering, it is everywhere to be seen.

There are probably as many versions of *panettone* as there are bakeries in Italy. The recipe given here is one adapted for bread machines. No recipe is given for a so-called large loaf, however, because the oblong pans of machines like the Panasonic have the wrong shape for it, while large loaves of it from machines like the Hitachi are simply too tall to cut without toppling.

SMALL

⅓ cup water

1 medium egg

2 egg yolks

2 tablespoons unsalted butter (or canola oil)

2 tablespoons grated orange or lemon zest

¼ cup chopped candied citron

1⅞ cups unbleached all-purpose flour

¼ to 1 teaspoon salt, to taste
1½ teaspoons active dry yeast
½ cup raisins

Remember that if the instructions that came with your bread machine call for the yeast to be placed in the baking pan first, the flour and salt should be added next, before the remaining ingredients. Otherwise, pour the water into your pan, then add the egg, egg yolks, butter (or canola oil), orange or lemon zest, citron, flour, salt, and yeast. If your machine has a separate dispenser for leavening, spoon the yeast into its slot after all the other ingredients have been measured into the baking pan.

Set your machine on its quick cycle. When it beeps a last call for ingredients, add the raisins. If your machine doesn't have a raisin alarm, add them 10 minutes into the first kneading cycle.

Panettone Farcito

It's not all that difficult to make *panettone farcito*, the legendary version of *panettone* laced with orange liqueur, stuffed with sweetened cheese, zest, and chocolate, and crowned with confectioners' sugar. It is demanding only in that it needs a few hours of undisturbed chilling in the refrigerator following its assembly. And it is something to behold! So if the loaf of *panettone* that emerges from your electronic oven happens to be perfectly shaped and fairly pleading to be treated specially, do give this creation a try.

You may be startled to note the chocolate chips, strongly associated with American baking, in this very Italian recipe. Well, if you want to hark back to the days before chocolate chips, you can substitute 2 one-ounce squares of semisweet baking chocolate, coarsely grated. But the chocolate's essentially the same, and tossing in the chips is so much easier!

After baking the *Panettone* (see above), prepare the filling.

1½ cups ricotta cheese
¼ cup confectioners' sugar
1 tablespoon grated orange zest
2 tablespoons cocoa
½ teaspoon vanilla extract
⅓ cup semisweet chocolate chips
(or 2 one-ounce squares of semi-
sweet baking chocolate, coarsely
grated)

orange liqueur for lacing the Panet-
tone (approximately ¼ cup)

confectioners' sugar for garnish

Scoop the ricotta cheese into a small bowl and, using an electric mixer, beat in the ¼ cup of confectioners' sugar. Spoon in the orange zest, cocoa, and vanilla extract and blend until the mixture is smooth and creamy. Fold in the chocolate chips (or grated chocolate).

To assemble the cake, first lay the freshly baked *Panettone* (see preceding recipe) on its side and, using a long, thin serrated knife with a good point, slice off the top crust and about an inch of the bottom of the loaf. Reserve. Then carefully cut a cylinder through the remaining bar of bread and gently remove this core, leaving a shell about 1 inch thick. Although perhaps daunting to contemplate, the maneuver is really not difficult to perform.

Cut the circular core crosswise into 4 even slices. Two of these rounds can be frozen for later use in a fondue or bread pudding. Set the other 2 aside for the moment.

Sprinkle both the reserved square cut from the bottom of the *Panettone* and the inside of the shell you've just created with about a third of the orange liqueur. Place the shell over the bottom piece

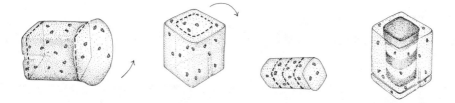

to form a drum. Spoon a third of the cheese mixture into this well. Then sprinkle both sides of one of the reserved rounds with a little more of the orange liqueur and insert it to form a layer of cake over the filling. Spoon in another third of the cheese mixture, sprinkle the second cake round with orange liqueur, and place it over this layer of filling. Add the remaining filling, then sprinkle the underside of the top crust of the *Panettone* with the remaining liqueur and place it over the shell of bread as a lid.

Chill the cake in the refrigerator for 3 to 4 hours before serving. Just before bringing the *Panettone Farcito* to the table, dust the top with confectioners' sugar. Cut vertically into wedges to serve.

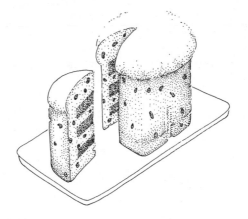

Pumpkin-Pie-Spice Loaf

This is one of those loaves whose components lend themselves to being loaded into the bread machine in the morning, with the timer set to produce a fresh, fragrant loaf as one walks in the door at the end of the day, without fear of the ingredients spoiling on even the warmest of days.

It's a simple, unpretentious loaf, light-textured and subtle in flavor, just a little spicy, just a little reminiscent of the apples of summer, just a little sweet, but mostly just a good homey bread.

SMALL

1 cup unsweetened chunky
  applesauce
2 tablespoons unsalted butter or
  canola oil
2 cups unbleached all-purpose flour
1/2 cup wheat bran
2 tablespoons dark brown sugar
1 1/2 teaspoons pumpkin-pie spice
1/2 to 1 teaspoon salt, to taste
1 1/2 teaspoons active dry yeast

LARGE

1 1/3 cups unsweetened chunky
  applesauce
3 tablespoons unsalted butter or
  canola oil
3 cups unbleached all-purpose flour
3/4 cup wheat bran
3 tablespoons dark brown sugar
2 teaspoons pumpkin-pie spice
1 to 2 teaspoons salt, to taste
2 teaspoons active dry yeast

Spoon the applesauce into the baking pan of your bread machine and add the butter or canola oil, flour, wheat bran, brown sugar, pumpkin-pie spice, salt, and yeast. Remember, however, to follow the directions that came with your particular machine in incorporating the leavening. If the yeast is to be placed in the pan first thing, then the applesauce and butter or canola oil should be reserved till last, and if the machine has a separate dispenser for leavening, that's where the yeast should go.

Select the machine's rapid-bake cycle for this bread. If desired, set the timer for a loaf whose just-baked fragrance will lift the spirits of any weary homecomer.

Ginger Cake

Back in the thirteenth and fourteenth centuries, when the trade in ginger was as lively as that in pepper, the sensual powers attributed to it certainly enhanced its sales. But it does seem curious that the spice most widely used in Chinese cookery should have come to be the archetypical Christmas flavor in the West. What's Christmas, after all, without gingersnaps or a gingerbread house?

Whatever the reasons for ginger's worldwide popularity, its wake-up flavor is indomitable. Slice this loaf very thin and spread it with sweet creamery butter for a quick, refreshing pick-me-up. For a more leisurely repast, try the striped gingerbread stack described below. The dark and light bands of cream cheese and lekvar, or prune butter, are striking, as is the subtle blend of flavors that results.

SMALL	LARGE
3/4 cup milk, whole or skim	*1 cup milk, whole or skim*
2 tablespoons heavy cream	*1/4 cup heavy cream*
3 tablespoons canola or other light oil	*1/4 cup canola or other light oil*
	1 medium egg
1 cup unbleached all-purpose flour	*2 cups unbleached all-purpose flour*
3/4 cup semolina flour	*1 1/2 cups semolina flour*
1/2 cup sugar	*2/3 cup sugar*
1 tablespoon instant coffee, regular or decaffeinated	*2 tablespoons instant coffee, regular or decaffeinated*
1 1/2 teaspoons ground ginger	*2 teaspoons ground ginger*
1 1/2 teaspoons ground cloves	*2 teaspoons ground cloves*
1/2 to 1 teaspoon salt, to taste	*1 to 2 teaspoons salt, to taste*
1 1/2 teaspoons active dry yeast	*2 teaspoons active dry yeast*

Pour the milk into your bread machine baking pan and add the cream and oil, along with the egg if you are making the large loaf. If the instructions that came with your machine specify that the yeast is to be placed in the bottom of the pan first thing, however, these ingredients should be reserved to be added last, after the dry ones. Measure in the all-purpose and semolina flours and add the sugar, instant coffee, ginger, cloves, salt, and yeast, spooning the leavening into its own dispenser if a separate container is provided for it on your machine.

Bake the loaf on your machine's quick cycle.

For a striped gingerbread stack, spectacular both to behold and to taste, remove all crusts but the top crust once the loaf has cooled. Lay the loaf on its side and cut it into slices about ½ inch thick. The bread can be sliced into even thinner pieces, which are nice for simply buttered tea sandwiches, but here you'll be stacking the layers, and you don't want the edifice to be too precarious.

Set the top crust aside and spread the other slices alternately with cream cheese and lekvar, or prune butter. (You'll need, for either the small or large loaf, 3 or 4 ounces of cream cheese, double that if you'd like a swirl of it whipped to crown the loaf, and a 12-ounce can or jar of prune filling — you don't want to run out just short of the top of the stack.) Apple butter, which also goes well with this loaf, can be substituted for the lekvar, but only if its consistency is very firm.

Smooth the filling all the way out to the edges of the slices. It's best to spread each slice while it's flat on your working surface and then add it to the stack, as if you were buttering an order of toast, rather than placing each slice on the stack and then spreading it with filling, as in assembling a layer cake. Don't worry about a little filling oozing over the edge of the bread.

Stack the layers like pancakes, run a knife around the perimeter of the stack to remove any excess filling and to bring out the striped

pattern, and put the upper crust in place. Add a swirled topknot of whipped cream cheese as the stack's crowning glory. If the cream cheese is difficult to whip, it can be softened with about 1 tablespoon of cream or milk. Sprinkle with chopped nuts or dates if desired.

Sour Cream Blueberry Loaf

Chantilly Cream

"Not again!" was Susan's first startled remark upon cutting open my first version of this thick, dark loaf. It's true, I have on occasion come up with a loaf whose color somehow did not jibe with Western society's gustatory norms. A blue corn bread that was vividly blue comes immediately to mind. Well, here was another blue loaf. This time the color resulted from dried blueberries — and the flavor was irresistible.

When it comes to baking, dried blueberries impart far more taste per spoonful than do fresh ones, even the ones straight from our blueberry patch. Particularly in a bread-machine dough, the moisture in fresh berries limits the amount you can use, so you can achieve only a fraction of the flavor found in a loaf using dried berries.

The trick in adding the flavor without the blue is to reserve the berries to toss into your bread machine pan after the initial kneading cycle. Some machines have a beep signal to let you know when such things as whole berries should be added.

SMALL	LARGE
1 cup sour cream or yogurt, regular or low-fat	*1½ cups sour cream or yogurt, regular or low-fat*
1 tablespoon unsalted butter or canola oil	*2 tablespoons unsalted butter or canola oil*
2 cups unbleached all-purpose flour	*2¾ cups unbleached all-purpose flour*
1 tablespoon dark brown sugar	*2 tablespoons dark brown sugar*
½ teaspoon ground allspice	*1 teaspoon ground allspice*
¼ to 1 teaspoon salt, to taste	*½ to 1½ teaspoons salt, to taste*
1½ teaspoons active dry yeast	*2 teaspoons active dry yeast*
⅓ cup dried blueberries	*½ cup dried blueberries*

Unless the instructions that came with your machine call for placing the yeast in the very bottom of the pan, followed by the other dry ingredients and then the liquids, spoon the sour cream or yogurt into your baking pan and add the butter or canola oil, flour, brown sugar, allspice, salt, and yeast, reserving the last for its own separate dispenser if your machine has one.

Set the machine to its rapid-bake cycle for this loaf, and don't forget to add the blueberries at the beep, or 10 minutes into the first kneading cycle if your machine doesn't beep for dried fruit.

For a tea cake that looks luscious — and is — remove the crusts from this loaf, slice it crosswise, cut the slices on the diagonal, spread them liberally with Chantilly Cream (see below) and fresh blueberries, and line them up in a row like a prism on a pretty platter. Even off the edges of the filling with the flat edge of a knife or a spatula and surround the cake with more blueberries, sugared or glazed with a little melted apple jelly if you'd like.

CHANTILLY CREAM

1 cup heavy cream, well chilled
1 tablespoon confectioners' sugar
1 teaspoon vanilla extract (or ½
teaspoon vanilla extract + ½
teaspoon almond extract)

Whip the cream, using chilled beaters and a chilled bowl, until it begins to thicken. Beat in the confectioners' sugar a little at a time. When the cream is almost stiff, add the vanilla extract (or the vanilla and almond extracts) and whip until blended. The touch of almond is scrumptious with blueberries, but vanilla alone works perfectly well.

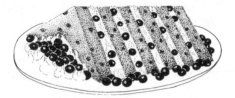

4 · Petits Fours and Other Frosted Treats

 THERE ARE TIMES when a sweet tooth really can't be satisfied with anything less than a richly frosted sweet. There's also something visually special about a thick, swirled icing or a glossy glaze on a dessert treat.

Now, the maximum amount of frosting per piece of cake is not found on those gorgeous big round layer cakes with the splendiferous frills on top. No, for the most frosting per bite, short of licking icing from the spoon after scraping out the mixing bowl — which, of course, is the baker's prerogative — what one wants is one of those little pastries known as petits fours. Here's an assemblage of these and other frosted delights.

Kumquat Delight

Easy Semisweet Chocolate Frosting

Kumquats aren't found only in Chinese restaurants or Oriental markets anymore. They are quite often available fresh in supermarkets throughout the country come late winter and early spring. When you see them, pick some up for this delightfully spicy, color-studded loaf.

Toasted slices of Kumquat Delight spread with sweet butter and Seville orange marmalade are a real breakfast treat. Slabs of the loaf edged or iced with chocolate, the rich frosting contrasting both in flavor and appearance with the handsome loaf itself, are a lovely accompaniment to an herbal or a fruit tea.

The pepper in the recipe, incidentally, didn't slip into the list of ingredients inadvertently. It does indeed belong there, for it accents the pungency of the kumquats.

SMALL
- ¾ cup milk, whole or skim
- 1 tablespoon unsalted butter (or canola oil)
- 1 cup fresh kumquats, halved and pitted
- 2½ cups unbleached all-purpose flour
- 2 tablespoons dark brown sugar
- 1 teaspoon ground mace
- ¼ teaspoon freshly ground black pepper
- ¼ to 1 teaspoon salt, to taste
- 1½ teaspoons active dry yeast

LARGE
- 1 cup milk
- 2 tablespoons unsalted butter (or canola oil)
- 1½ cups fresh kumquats, halved and pitted
- 3½ cups unbleached all-purpose flour
- 3 tablespoons dark brown sugar
- 1½ teaspoons ground mace
- ½ teaspoon freshly ground black pepper
- ½ to 1½ teaspoons salt, to taste
- 2 teaspoons active dry yeast

Pour the milk into your baking pan and add the butter (or canola oil), kumquats, flour, brown sugar, mace, pepper, and salt. Last, add the yeast, following the instructions given for your particular machine. If the model you have features a separate dispenser for leavening, add the yeast there. On the other hand, if the instructions for your machine specify that the leavening is to be placed in the baking pan first thing, reverse the order in which you add the liquids and the other dry ingredients.

Bake the loaf on your machine's quick cycle.

For the iced version of this loaf, let the Kumquat Delight cool on a rack for about 10 to 15 minutes after you've shaken it out of its pan. When it can be handled easily, cut it into fairly thick slices and, using a thin, flexible knife or spatula, spread a liberal helping of chocolate —either a commercial or a homemade spread — around the edges of the slabs. If you're a real chocolate fancier, spread it all over the tops too. Nutella, that wonderful chocolate-hazelnut spread imported from Italy, is another scrumptious choice. A chocolate icing no sweeter than semisweet, like the one below, best complements the kumquat flavor.

EASY SEMISWEET CHOCOLATE FROSTING

1 cup semisweet chocolate chips
2 cups heavy cream, well chilled
1 teaspoon vanilla extract
dash salt

kumquats for garnish

Melt the chocolate chips in a heavy saucepan over very low heat or in the top of a double boiler. Let the melted chocolate cool while you whip the cream, using a chilled bowl and beaters, until it is stiff and swirled. Stir the vanilla extract and salt into the melted chocolate and fold this mixture into the whipped cream. Spread to your heart's desire.

Garnish your Kumquat Delight with slices of kumquat or maybe even a whole fruit fanned out in a bold design. For a kumquat fan, cut the fruit lengthwise in thin slices almost all the way through to the

stem end. Setting the kumquat stem end down on a small lid like that of a vanilla extract bottle, as if you were placing it in an egg cup, helps you to keep from slicing too far. Then coax the slices apart sideways to open up the fan.

For a fabulous company display, cut slices of this bread in half and arrange them one edged up on the next in an overlapping row down the length of a serving platter. The bits of bright kumquat and rich chocolate on parade will be irresistible. Complete the enticement with sliced or fanned fruit as above, strewn with julienned kumquat for an extra splash of color.

Banana Almond Loaf

Basic Petit Four Icing

Here's an incredible fruit-and-nut combination. The almonds add both crunchiness and their own special flavor to this banana lover's delight, whose taste is accentuated by the extra splash of almond extract in the bread (a tip borrowed from a devastatingly rich banana cream pie Susan's mother used to make). For best results, wait until the bananas are really ripe before making this loaf.

"Ugh, they're black," Tanya once pointed out on seeing some poised on the counter by the bread machine awaiting further mellowing.

"Properly speckled to indicate ripeness," I corrected. True enough, for eating out of hand the bananas were a bit gone by. But I noticed there was no leftover Banana Almond Loaf to go stale.

Another flavor tip is to toast the almonds slightly before adding them to the dough. It's an optional step, but browning them on a cookie sheet in a 350-degree F. oven or in a dry skillet on the stovetop before using them really brings out their flavor.

You'll note from the recipe that this is a yeast-based, cakelike bread, not the more usual baking-powder banana nut bread. It makes an excellent base for petits fours.

SMALL	LARGE
1/4 cup milk, whole or skim	1/3 cup milk, whole or skim
1 tablespoon canola or other light oil	2 tablespoons canola or other light oil
1 medium egg	1 medium egg
1 cup mashed ripe banana	1 1/2 cups mashed ripe banana
1 teaspoon almond extract	1 1/2 teaspoons almond extract
1/2 cup slivered blanched almonds, toasted if desired	3/4 cup slivered blanched almonds, toasted if desired
2 1/2 cups unbleached all-purpose flour	3 1/2 cups unbleached all-purpose flour
1/4 cup dark brown sugar	1/3 cup dark brown sugar
1/4 to 1 teaspoon salt, to taste	1/2 to 1 1/2 teaspoons salt, to taste
1 1/2 teaspoons active dry yeast	2 teaspoons active dry yeast

Measure the milk and oil into the baking pan of your bread machine and break the egg into it. Add the mashed banana, almond extract, almonds, flour, brown sugar, salt, and, last — unless the instructions for your particular machine direct you to reverse the order in which you add the dry and the liquid ingredients — the yeast. If your machine has a separate dispenser for leavening, spoon the yeast in there.

Select the machine's rapid-bake cycle for this loaf.

A commercial frosting can be used to ice a Banana Almond Loaf, but if you'd like to make petits fours, here's a basic, simple, uncooked icing that will make delectable ones.

BASIC PETIT FOUR ICING

2 cups confectioners' sugar
1 tablespoon unsalted butter, soft-
ened
¼ cup water, lemon or orange
juice, strong coffee, or other liq-
uid of your choice
1 teaspoon vanilla or other extract
a few drops food coloring (op-
tional)
assorted nuts, fresh fruit, and mint
leaves for garnish

In a small bowl, blend the confectioners' sugar, butter, and, start-ing with a small amount and adding it gradually, the water, juice, coffee, or other liquid. Add the vanilla or other extract and the food coloring if desired. Beat the mixture until it is very smooth, adding more liquid if necessary. The icing should be thin enough to be poured, even though you're not actually going to pour it, but not so diluted that it will simply run off the cake squares. If the icing be-comes too thin, simply add more confectioners' sugar until the right consistency for spreading is reached. If it becomes too stiff, just add more liquid. You can't ruin this icing.

In its most basic form, petit four icing uses for the necessary mois-ture plain tap water and, if something a little flashier than a plain white frosting is desired, a drop or two of food coloring. But any liquid can be substituted for the water to add both color and flavor. Besides coffee and fruit juices, you can use syrup drained from canned fruit, maple syrup, chocolate syrup — the possible variations on this basic recipe are almost limitless.

To assemble the petits fours, first trim the crusts from your Banana Almond Loaf. If you trim them generously so a little of the moist inner part goes with them, these outer slices can be frozen for later use in a fondue. They complement a butterscotch fondue nicely.

Cut the remaining block into 1- to 2-inch cubes. Spear the cubes with a fork one by one and dip them into the bowl holding the icing.

When they are well coated on all sides but the bottom, ease them off onto a rack to dry.

Wait half an hour for the icing to set, then decorate the top of each petit four with a single strawberry, raspberry, or nut resting against a fresh mint leaf. Arranging the squares on individual small doilies will not only add a dainty touch, but will make serving the petits fours easier as well.

Sweet Peppermint Poppy Seed Loaf

Peppermint Petit Four Icing

Poppy seeds scattered lightly over rolls or bagels, a decorative touch in miniature black pointillism on a glazed crust, are a familiar sight in this country. Rarely are they seen in more concentrated numbers, however. Yet in some European countries poppy seeds are widely used as a flavoring agent.

Something like poppy seed strudel is at best an acquired taste for most of us. But here's a moist, cakelike loaf distinctively peppered all over with poppy seeds, inside and out, that's bound to please just about everyone. Cube it and ice it with a pepperminty frosting, petit-four style, or serve it sliced for tea with a little jug of peppermint or orange butter — simply cream ½ cup softened unsalted butter with

1 tablespoon confectioners' sugar and your preference of ½ tea-spoon of either peppermint or orange extract.

SMALL	LARGE
1 cup sour cream or yogurt, regular or low-fat	*1⅓ cups sour cream or yogurt, regular or low-fat*
2 tablespoons unsalted butter or canola oil	*3 tablespoons unsalted butter or canola oil*
1 tablespoon honey	*2 tablespoons honey*
1 teaspoon peppermint extract	*1½ teaspoons peppermint extract*
⅓ cup canned poppy seed filling	*½ cup canned poppy seed filling*
2 cups unbleached all-purpose flour	*3 cups unbleached all-purpose flour*
¼ cup cornmeal	*⅓ cup cornmeal*
¼ to 1 teaspoon salt, to taste	*½ to 1½ teaspoons salt, to taste*
1½ teaspoons active dry yeast	*2½ teaspoons active dry yeast*

Scoop the sour cream or yogurt into your bread machine baking pan and add the butter or canola oil, honey, peppermint extract, poppy seed filling, flour, cornmeal, and salt. Add the yeast as directed for your machine. Remember to reverse the order of ingredients if so instructed by the manufacturer's guidelines.

Use your machine's quick cycle for this loaf.

PEPPERMINT PETIT FOUR ICING

2 cups confectioners' sugar
1 tablespoon unsalted butter, soft-ened
¼ cup water
½ teaspoon peppermint extract

crushed peppermint candies for gar-nish

Measure the confectioners' sugar into a bowl, add the butter and a little of the water, and cream to a smooth paste. Continue adding water, a little at a time, beating until the icing is of a good dipping consistency. Blend in the peppermint extract.

Petits Fours and Other Frosted Treats ❖ *43*

Petits fours dipped in this icing are attractively garnished with bits of bright peppermint candies scattered over the top.

Coffee Nips Coffee Cake

Mocha Buttercream Icing

Why coffee cakes never tasted of coffee was one of those minor mysteries of my childhood long unresolved. That the name derived from the association of the cakes with the coffee they so often accompanied somehow never entered my juvenile mind, probably because I would consume them at any opportunity granted, *sans* coffee.

Here's a coffee cake that's distinctly coffee-flavored, twice so if spread with the Mocha Buttercream Icing that follows the cake recipe. The loaf is silky, soft, moist, and flavorsome. Served simply with butter, it's not as sweet as one might expect from a perusal of the ingredients. Slices iced with the mocha frosting, on the other hand, make a rich nibble indeed.

SMALL

⅞ cup milk, whole or skim
3 tablespoons unsalted butter (or canola oil)
1 medium egg
1 teaspoon coffee extract
1 cup unbleached all-purpose flour
1 cup semolina flour
½ cup graham cracker crumbs
½ cup sugar
⅓ cup instant Viennese chocolate coffee
1 tablespoon instant coffee, regular or decaffeinated
2 teaspoons active dry yeast

LARGE

1¼ cups milk, whole or skim
⅓ cup unsalted butter (or canola oil)
1 medium egg
1½ teaspoons coffee extract
1⅔ cups unbleached all-purpose flour
1½ cups semolina flour
¾ cup graham cracker crumbs
⅔ cup sugar
½ cup instant Viennese chocolate coffee
2 tablespoons instant coffee, regular or decaffeinated
2½ teaspoons active dry yeast

Remember that if the instructions that came with your bread machine call for the yeast to be placed in the baking pan first, the dry ingredients should be added before the liquids. Otherwise, pour the milk into your pan and add the butter (or canola oil), egg, and coffee extract. Then measure in the all-purpose and semolina flours, graham cracker crumbs, sugar, instant Viennese chocolate coffee, and instant coffee. Last, add the yeast, placing it in its own separate dispenser if your machine has one.

Set the machine to its rapid-bake cycle for this loaf.

While a Coffee Nips loaf really needs no accompaniment as a tea or coffee cake, it also lends itself to more decorative treatment for festive occasions. Slice the bread in fairly thick pieces and cut each slice into four triangles, canapé style. Spread the triangles with Mocha Buttercream Icing and garnish each with chocolate coffee beans.

MOCHA BUTTERCREAM ICING

> ¼ cup heavy cream, well chilled
> ¼ cup instant coffee, regular or de-
>   caffeinated, dissolved in ¼ cup
>   cold water
> ¼ cup unsalted butter, softened
> 3 cups confectioners' sugar
> 1 teaspoon coffee extract
> 1 teaspoon chocolate extract
> 1 teaspoon vanilla extract
>
> chocolate coffee beans for garnish

Pour the cream and the dissolved instant coffee into a small mixing bowl, add the butter and 1 cup of the confectioners' sugar, and beat well. Beat in 1 more cup of the confectioners' sugar and then the coffee, chocolate, and vanilla extracts. Add the remaining 1 cup of confectioners' sugar and beat at high speed for 3 to 4 minutes (don't overbeat or the cream may separate) or until the icing is light and fluffy. Spread immediately and garnish with chocolate coffee beans.

Any extra buttercream can be frozen for another day. Simply defrost it as needed, and while it's still quite cold, whip it again for a couple of minutes to fluff it up once more.

Triple Chocolate Loaf

White Buttercream Icing

Chocolate is a flavor that seems particularly difficult to capture with a bread machine. In my quest for a truly chocolaty loaf, I keep experimenting with more and more of it. What I'm striving for is not the ultimate in devastatingly rich chocolate-frosted devil's food cakes, although I'm as much a sucker for those as any chocolate lover. No, what I have in mind is one of those chocolate cakes that are rich but not so sugary that the chocolate is overpowered.

Here's a dense, fine-grained, cakelike chocolate loaf that combines the subtly different triple flavors of cocoa, hot fudge sauce, and chocolate extract. For those who like it sweet, try the White Buttercream Icing that follows the loaf recipe. Freeze any extra pieces of the loaf for a chocolate or a mocha fondue some other day.

SMALL	LARGE
⅓ cup milk, whole or skim	*½ cup milk, whole or skim*
¼ cup unsalted butter (or canola oil)	*6 tablespoons (¾ stick) unsalted butter (or canola oil)*
1 medium egg	*1 medium egg*
1 tablespoon unheated hot fudge sauce	*2 tablespoons unheated hot fudge sauce*
1 tablespoon lemon juice	*2 tablespoons lemon juice*
1 teaspoon vanilla extract	*2 teaspoons vanilla extract*
1 teaspoon chocolate extract	*1½ teaspoons chocolate extract*
2 cups unbleached all-purpose flour	*3 cups unbleached all-purpose flour*
¼ cup sugar	*⅓ cup sugar*
¼ cup cocoa	*⅓ cup cocoa*
1 tablespoon instant coffee, regular or decaffeinated	*2 tablespoons instant coffee, regular or decaffeinated*
¼ to 1 teaspoon salt, to taste	*½ to 1½ teaspoons salt, to taste*
1½ teaspoons active dry yeast	*2 teaspoons active dry yeast*

Pour the milk into your baking pan, unless the instructions for your machine direct you to place the yeast in the bottom of the pan first thing, in which case the other dry ingredients should be added next, the liquids last. Add the butter (or canola oil). Since a sizable quantity of butter is involved, if yours is still cold from the refrigerator, cut it into chunks before adding it to the milk, to ensure its blending evenly with the other ingredients. Break the egg into the pan and add the hot fudge sauce, lemon juice, and vanilla and chocolate extracts. Measure in the flour, sugar, cocoa, instant coffee, salt, and yeast, placing the leavening in its own separate dispenser if your machine has that device.

To bake the loaf, set the machine to its rapid cycle.

The Triple Chocolate Loaf is fine just plain or lightly buttered still warm from its pan. It's also lovely iced, however. Crown its low top with thick swirls of White Buttercream Icing (set the butter out to soften when you turn on the bread machine, and the icing will be quickly made), or cut the loaf into slices or cubes and ice the individual pieces, cupcake or petit four style. Of course, when you cover the sides too, the visual contrast between the dark chocolate and the white buttercream is lost — until you bite into a piece.

WHITE BUTTERCREAM ICING

¹/₄ cup heavy cream, well chilled
¹/₄ cup unsalted butter, softened
2 cups confectioners' sugar
1 teaspoon vanilla extract

cocoa for garnish

Pour the cream into a small mixing bowl, add the butter and 1 cup of the confectioners' sugar, and beat well. Add the remaining 1 cup of confectioners' sugar and the vanilla extract and beat at high speed for 3 to 5 minutes (just don't overbeat, lest the cream separate) or until the icing is light and easy to spread.

Individual servings of this treat are prettily decorated with cocoa dusted over the top through a paper doily.

Freeze any unused portion of the buttercream for future use. When needed, it can simply be defrosted and whipped up while still cold for a couple of minutes again.

Rose and Orange Loaf

Rose Water Glaze

Flower waters, quaint by today's Western culinary standards, have been popular flavorings for millennia in the Near East. The Turkish delight so popular in this country at the turn of the century was originally none other than bite-size bits of flower-flavored jellies dusted in confectioners' sugar.

In England, these fruit flavorings gained immense popularity during the Crusades, when those returning from the Holy Land brought home rose and orange flower waters. For a couple of hundred years, right into the reign of Queen Victoria, these flavorings were as popular as vanilla is today.

Considering that vanilla is derived from the dried seedpod of an orchid, why should rose flavoring seem so strange? I asked Revell.

"What, eat perfume?" he retorted.

Logic sometimes does not work with a twelve-year-old.

In point of fact, the flavor of rose may not work for you either. But try it, at least. The loaf is soft and white, with a cookielike crust, and the flavor is wonderfully delicate. Remarkably, the rose water is not overpowered by the lemon juice. The cake's elusive taste can be accentuated with Rose Water Glaze, which follows the loaf recipe.

One note: when purchasing rose water for cooking, make sure that what you buy is culinary-grade rose water.

SMALL	LARGE
½ cup milk, whole or skim	¾ cup milk, whole or skim
3 tablespoons unsalted butter	¼ cup unsalted butter
2 tablespoons solid vegetable shortening	3 tablespoons solid vegetable shortening
1 tablespoon rose water	4½ teaspoons rose water
1 tablespoon orange water	4½ teaspoons orange water
1 tablespoon lemon juice	4½ teaspoons lemon juice
2 cups unbleached all-purpose flour	3 cups unbleached all-purpose flour
¼ cup sugar	⅓ cup sugar
¼ to ½ teaspoon salt, to taste	½ to 1 teaspoon salt, to taste
1½ teaspoons active dry yeast	2 teaspoons active dry yeast

If the directions for your bread machine instruct you to place the yeast in the very bottom of the baking pan, you will need to reverse the order in which you incorporate the liquid and the dry ingredients. Otherwise, pour the milk into your pan and add the butter. If you are making the large loaf and using butter still cold from the refrigerator, cut it into pieces to facilitate its blending with the other ingredients. Measure in the shortening, rose and orange waters, lemon juice, flour, sugar, salt, and yeast. Where a separate dispenser is provided for leavening, spoon the yeast in there.

Bake the loaf on your machine's quick cycle.

In *The Compleat Cook*, a compendium of recipes from the late sixteenth and early seventeenth centuries, there appears the following recipe for a rose water sugar glaze: "Against you draw the cake from the Oven have some Rose Water and Sugar finely beaten, and well mixed together to wash the upper side of it, then set it in the Oven to dry out, when you draw it out, it will shew like Ice."

Here's my adaptation. For best results, spread it while your loaf is still warm—but not hot—from its baking pan.

ROSE WATER GLAZE

> 1 tablespoon rose water
> 1 tablespoon heavy cream
> 1½ cups confectioners' sugar

Combine the rose water and cream in a small bowl and stir in enough of the confectioners' sugar to form a smooth paste. Beat in additional confectioners' sugar a little at a time until the glaze is of a good consistency for spreading. If the glazing mixture becomes too thick, add an extra splash of cream.

It's true that they didn't use cream for this glaze in Shakespeare's time. Then again, they didn't use electric mixers in those days either. The cream acts as a binder and helps to smooth the glaze, which does indeed add sparkle to the top of the loaf.

Luau Loaf

Most of the macadamia nuts we buy in our local supermarkets come from Hawaii, as do, of course, a lot of pineapples. Hence the name for this tasty, soft, light-textured loaf. For extra pineapple flavor, when you drain the pineapple rings called for in the recipe, reserve the syrup in which they were packed to boil down and use as a glaze on the finished loaf.

SMALL	LARGE
½ cup heavy cream	*⅔ cup heavy cream*
¼ cup canola or other light oil	*⅓ cup canola or other light oil*
1 teaspoon pineapple extract	*1½ teaspoons pineapple extract*
½ teaspoon orange extract	*¾ teaspoon orange extract*
¼ to ½ teaspoon coconut extract, to taste	*½ to ¾ teaspoon coconut extract, to taste*
5 canned pineapple rings, drained, liquid reserved for glazing loaf if desired	*8 canned pineapple rings, drained, liquid reserved for glazing loaf if desired*
1 cup dry-roasted macadamia nuts	*1½ cups dry-roasted macadamia nuts*
2¼ cups unbleached all-purpose flour	*3¼ cups unbleached all-purpose flour*
¼ to 1 teaspoon salt, to taste	*½ to 1½ teaspoons salt, to taste*
1½ teaspoons active dry yeast	*2 teaspoons active dry yeast*

Pour the cream and oil into your baking pan and add the pineapple, orange, and coconut extracts, pineapple rings, macadamia nuts, flour, salt, and yeast, placing the leavening in its own separate dispenser if your machine has such a device. If, on the other hand, the instructions that came with your machine specify that the yeast is to be placed in the very bottom of the pan first thing, remember to reverse the order in which you add the liquid and the dry ingredients.

Set the machine to its rapid-bake cycle for this loaf.

While the Luau Loaf is baking, you can make an attractive glaze with which to crown it when it emerges from the electronic oven. Reduce the pineapple syrup reserved from draining the canned pineapple slices by two thirds, boiling it down in a small saucepan. Using a pastry brush, paint the hot loaf as soon as you've taken it from its baking pan with this thickened syrup. For a pretty contrast that will also enhance the flavor of the loaf, sprinkle shredded coconut over the glaze before it has set.

If you just happen to have a chunk of fresh coconut tucked away in the refrigerator, you can make an even more spectacular garnish by paring delicate strips of coconut from the chunk with a vegetable peeler, much as you would pare chocolate curls from a square of semisweet baking chocolate, and then arranging the strips in careless curls atop the glazed loaf. Handle gently, since the curls will not only look, but be, very delicate.

Double Almond Loaf

Quick No-Fail Creamy Hot Fudge Sauce

Supporting my theory that one really can't have a surfeit of almonds when it comes to baking — the more I experiment with almond loaves, the more of these nuts I keep adding in one form or another — here's a recipe that uses both almond paste or marzipan and the nut in its more crunchy, slivered form.

With all that almond paste in it, along with the milk needed to help soften it, the dough for this bread is very moist, which is why there is no separate recipe for a large version of it. A bread machine with a large oblong pan for its loaf would encounter rather unmanageable difficulties, with the greater mass of dough sticking in the corners. A machine with a tall pan for its large loaf would avoid that pitfall, but such a machine will also accommodate the smaller batch, and as you'll see, the recipe given here will result in an amply sized loaf, high-domed and altogether lovely.

SMALL

1 cup milk, whole or skim

*2 tablespoons unsalted butter (or
canola oil)*

1 medium egg

*7 ounces almond paste or marzi-
pan, coarsely chopped if firm*

*¹/₃ cup slivered blanched almonds,
toasted for accentuated flavor if
desired*

*2¹/₂ cups unbleached all-purpose
flour*

2 tablespoons dark brown sugar

¹/₄ to ¹/₂ teaspoon salt, to taste

1¹/₂ teaspoons active dry yeast

Unless the instructions that came with your machine call for placing the yeast in the very bottom of your baking pan, followed by the
other dry ingredients and then the liquids, pour the milk into the pan
and add the butter (or canola oil), egg, almond paste or marzipan,
almonds, flour, brown sugar, salt, and yeast, reserving the last for its
own separate dispenser if your machine has one.

Select your machine's quick cycle for this loaf and take a peek
inside the machine to check on the activity about 5 or 10 minutes
into the first kneading cycle, since the dough tends to be quite moist
and sticky initially. It may be necessary to scrape down the sides of
the pan to make sure that all the bits are incorporated.

Susan, who is not only an almond fancier but a puzzle enthusiast as
well, combined the two interests in coming up with a way to convert
the rectangular loaf of this bread that our machine turns out into a
prism-shaped cake that's become known in our house as the Strawberry Ridge, a confection filled with strawberry preserves, covered
with hot fudge sauce, and garnished with ripe strawberries. Its assembly takes only a few minutes, really, particularly if you microwave the hot fudge sauce to warm it.

Lay the loaf on its side and trim off the top and bottom crusts.

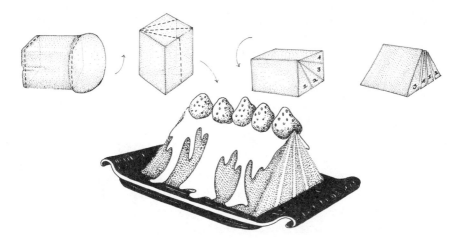

Freeze these, tightly wrapped, and you'll have the makings of excellent cubes for a chocolate or butterscotch fondue someday.

Next, return the trimmed loaf to an upright position and slice it in half diagonally from top to bottom so that you have 2 right-angled triangles. Now, keeping the loaf together, cut each triangle in half again, starting from the same corner. This will give you 4 triangles, the 2 center ones of which will be, if you remember your geometry, obtuse ones.

Still holding the loaf together, gently lay it on its side again and flip 2 triangles from one side over to the other side, forming a prism. Separate the wedges enough to spread them with the strawberry preserves, then press them together again.

Pour hot fudge sauce the length of the ridge, letting it flow down the sides, and perch a row of strawberries along the top line.

Another popular version of this cake in our house is a ridge filled with almond paste or marzipan and covered with whipped cream before the strawberries are hoisted into place. Now there's a rich cake!

QUICK NO-FAIL CREAMY HOT FUDGE SAUCE

1 fourteen-ounce can sweetened
condensed milk
2 one-ounce squares unsweetened
baking chocolate
2 tablespoons unsalted butter
2 teaspoons vanilla extract

Scoop the sweetened condensed milk into a heavy saucepan or the top of a double boiler. Add the chocolate and stir over low heat until the chocolate has melted completely and the mixture is thick and smooth. Add the butter, stirring quickly until it is blended into the sauce. Remove the pan from the heat and add the vanilla extract.

"Tastes like melted brownies" is Revell's assessment of this sauce.

Cranberry-Orange Loaf

Quick Orange Glaze

The flavor of cranberries and oranges combined is a uniquely American one. Although wild cranberries are popular in Europe and Russia, in neither area is there a counterpart to the vast cultivated cranberry bogs that dot the sandier areas of coastal New England. As to oranges, well, Floridians may complain about the occasional freeze, but have they ever tried growing citrus fruits in Siberia?

The recipe presented here uses dried cranberries. Their concentrated flavor adds a much more intense accent to the loaf than one could hope to achieve in a bread machine using fresh berries. Also, because the dried cranberries are quite firm, it's possible to simply toss them into the baking pan with all the other ingredients, instead of waiting to add them until after the dough has been mixed and kneaded, and still have whole chunks of delectable berries scattered throughout the finished loaf. Fresh berries subjected to the battering of the kneading blade of a bread machine are mushed into nothingness.

Dubbed by Susan the Constant Comment loaf because of its resemblance to that citrus-accented tea, this one makes lovely petits fours to hide under a lemony or orange-flavored icing or glaze, such as the one following the loaf recipe.

SMALL	LARGE
¾ cup milk, whole or skim	1 cup milk, whole or skim
3 tablespoons unsalted butter	¼ cup unsalted butter
2 tablespoons solid vegetable shortening	3 tablespoons solid vegetable shortening
1 tablespoon orange extract	1½ tablespoons orange extract
1 tablespoon grated orange zest	4½ teaspoons grated orange zest
⅓ cup dried cranberries	½ cup dried cranberries
2½ cups unbleached all-purpose flour	3¼ cups unbleached all-purpose flour
¼ cup sugar	⅓ cup sugar
¼ to 1 teaspoon salt, to taste	½ to 1½ teaspoons salt, to taste
1½ teaspoons active dry yeast	2 teaspoons active dry yeast

Pour the milk into your baking pan and add the butter, cut into chunks if you are making the larger loaf so it will blend more easily with the other ingredients. Measure in the shortening, orange extract, orange zest, cranberries, flour, sugar, salt, and yeast, placing the leavening in its own dispenser if your machine has one. If the instructions that came with your model call for starting with the yeast, however, remember to reverse the order in which you add the liquids and the other dry ingredients.

To bake the loaf, use your machine's quick cycle.

> 2 tablespoons unsalted butter
> juice and grated zest of 1 small
>   orange
> 3 cups confectioners' sugar
>
> julienned orange zest and/or cran-
>   berries, fresh or dried, for garnish

Melt the butter in a small saucepan. Stir in the orange juice and zest, then gradually blend in the confectioners' sugar until the glaze is of a good dipping consistency. Let stand for 5 minutes before dipping the petits fours, preferably while the cubes are still slightly warm, and allow them to drain on a cake rack until the glaze is set.

Julienned orange zest adds an attractive finish to petits fours dipped in this glaze. If you don't mind giving away the secret of the little cakes inside, add a dried or fresh cranberry or two to the arrangement.

Chocolate Nut Delight

Dark Chocolate Icing

Chocolate and nuts just go together, and here's a loaf that incorporates generous quantities of both. With the addition of a simple chocolate frosting (see the recipe following the one for the loaf), you can create from it a delicious mock *Rehrücken*, a German torte baked in a long half-round tin, turned out, and iced. This traditional hunting-country dessert is decorated with rows of almonds along its top to resemble the larding strips for the saddle of venison it is meant to imitate.

SMALL	LARGE
1 cup milk, whole or skim	*1½ cups milk, whole or skim*
2 tablespoons canola or other light oil	*3 tablespoons canola or other light oil*
¼ cup unsulfured molasses	*⅓ cup unsulfured molasses*
1 teaspoon chocolate extract	*1½ teaspoons chocolate extract*
¼ cup almonds	*⅓ cup almonds*
¼ cup hazelnuts	*⅓ cup hazelnuts*
¼ cup pecans	*⅓ cup pecans*
2 cups unbleached all-purpose flour	*3¼ cups unbleached all-purpose flour*
¼ cup cocoa	*⅓ cup cocoa*
¼ to 1 teaspoon salt, to taste	*½ to 1½ teaspoons salt, to taste*
2 teaspoons active dry yeast	*2½ teaspoons active dry yeast*

Unless the instructions for your machine specify that the yeast should be placed in the baking pan first thing, followed by the other dry ingredients and then the liquids, pour the milk, oil, and molasses into your baking pan and add the chocolate extract. Toss in the almonds, hazelnuts, and pecans and measure in the flour, cocoa, salt, and, last, the yeast. If your machine has a separate dispenser for leavening, add the yeast there.

Bake the loaf on your machine's quick cycle.

DARK CHOCOLATE ICING

8 one-ounce squares semisweet baking chocolate
½ cup unsalted butter, softened or cut into small chunks
1 teaspoon vanilla extract

whole or sliced blanched almonds for garnish

Place the chocolate in the top of a double boiler or in a heavy saucepan set over very low heat. Do not stir. When the chocolate is soft but not yet altogether liquid, remove from the heat and add the butter, stirring until melted. Blend in the vanilla extract.

To form the mock *Rehrücken,* cut the finished Chocolate Nut Delight in half lengthwise. If yours is a round bread machine pan, the loaf can simply be sliced down the center and the 2 halves laid end to end to make a long Quonset-hut-shaped cake, the traditional shape of this treat. A square cake is best cut on the diagonal. The 2 triangles can be similarly laid end to end to form a long prism.

Ice the cake and, if it's a rounded one, lay 3 rows of blanched almonds, either whole or sliced, along its top to form white stripes against the dark chocolate. Garnish a prism-shaped cake with a roof ridge of the almonds. Either way, the effect is stunning.

5 · Perrie's Delight and Other à la Modes

DURING MY EARLY TEENAGE YEARS, my family would eat out every couple of weeks at a now-defunct establishment called Perrie's. A neon Eiffel Tower flashed on a sign over the entrance, and the food was very Continental. They even served snails for appetizers, I would tell my startled classmates.

But it wasn't the escargots I reveled in. No, what I looked forward to in eager anticipation was a dessert called Perrie's Delight. It consisted of a slice of toasted pound cake topped by vanilla ice cream, hot fudge sauce, whipped cream, and, of course — this was the fifties, after all — a large maraschino cherry.

There's no way to make a good pound cake in any of the present generation of bread machines, so a true replica of the Perrie's Delight I knew is not possible in the bread machine bakery. However, employing the same principle, similar accessories, and a Butterscotch Brickle, Banana Chocolate, or Peanut Butter–Chocolate Chip Loaf, one can come up with an equally devastating dessert à la mode in next to no time.

Butterscotch Brickle Loaf

Almond Praline Cream

Butterscotch is one of those flavors that fall into the category of the sublime, and here's a quickly and easily made loaf that gains its blissful flavor from those bits of brickle found almost everywhere on grocery shelves under the name Bits 'O Brickle.

For bits in the finished bread true to their original size, add the brickles at the end of the first kneading cycle or at the beep with which some machines signal the moment to add whole raisins and whatnot. Simply tossing the brickles in with the other ingredients at the outset will give you an equally delectable and delightfully fragrant loaf, but the butterscotch flavor will be dispersed throughout the bread. That's okay too, if you don't mind skipping the textural contrast of biting into those little nuggets of caramelized crunch.

Lightly toasted slices of this bread are heavenly with French vanilla ice cream, topped by — what else? — hot butterscotch. A rich, creamy, homemade almond praline sauce (see the recipe following the one for the loaf), easy to whip up in advance and tuck away in the refrigerator till needed, adds a particularly opulent touch to this dish.

SMALL	LARGE
⅞ *cup milk, whole or skim*	1¼ *cups milk, whole or skim*
3 *tablespoons unsalted butter (or canola oil)*	¼ *cup unsalted butter (or canola oil)*
2 *teaspoons unsulfured molasses*	1 *tablespoon unsulfured molasses*
2 *cups unbleached all-purpose flour*	3 *cups unbleached all-purpose flour*
½ *cup graham cracker crumbs*	½ *cup graham cracker crumbs*
¼ *to 1 teaspoon salt, to taste*	½ *to 1½ teaspoons salt, to taste*
2 *teaspoons active dry yeast*	2½ *teaspoons active dry yeast*
¾ *cup butterscotch brickles*	1 *cup butterscotch brickles*

Pour the milk into the baking pan of your bread machine and add the butter (or canola oil), molasses, flour, graham cracker crumbs, salt, and yeast, placing the leavening in its own separate dispenser if your machine has one. Remember, however, that if the instructions accompanying your model call for placing the leavening in the bottom of the pan first thing, then the other dry ingredients should be added next, before the milk and butter (or canola oil).

Set your machine to its rapid-bake cycle for this loaf, and toss in the butterscotch brickles at the beep or after the first kneading.

To serve à la mode, toast slices of the loaf lightly to bring out their flavor, heap them with French vanilla ice cream, and ladle a liberal measure of hot butterscotch sauce over each helping. The toppings available commercially are fine, but for a real taste treat, try the Almond Praline Cream below.

ALMOND PRALINE CREAM

½ cup (1 stick) unsalted butter
2 cups firmly packed dark brown
*   sugar*
2 teaspoons lemon juice
2 cups heavy cream
3 tablespoons toasted blanched al-
*   monds*

Melt the butter in a heavy saucepan set over very low heat. Remove from the heat and add the brown sugar, creaming the mixture to a smooth paste. Add the lemon juice and mix well. Stir in the cream, return the pan to the stove, bring the sauce to a boil, and allow it to cook without stirring for 3 to 5 minutes or until a knife dipped in the syrup comes out very thickly coated. Just before serving, toss in the toasted almonds. The contrast between the crunchy nuts and the smooth butterscotch cream is wonderful.

Cherry Milk Loaf

The dried cherries that have recently become available at gourmet and bake shops are a real boon for bread machine enthusiasts. In an attempt to impart the piquant flavor of cherries to a yeast-based tea bread, I spent a lot of time experimenting with cherry pie fillings, cherry jams, and fresh cherries. The inevitable result was failure. The high sugar content of the pie fillings and jams simply overwhelmed the yeast required as the leavener in almost all bread machine baking, because the machines can't manage to whip eggs and don't handle quick breads reliably. Fresh cherries, which would seem the most elegant solution to the problem — discounting the messy job of pitting them all — simply don't add the concentrated fruit essence needed to create a loaf that is identifiably a cherry one.

Dried cherries, on the other hand, particularly the Montmorencies from Washington State, provide an incredible burst of flavor for their size. Add them after the machine's first kneading, or at the beep if your model features that signaling device, and you'll have a luscious loaf with a golden crust and bright cherries throughout.

SMALL
- 1/2 cup milk, whole or skim
- 3 tablespoons unsalted butter (or canola oil)
- 1 tablespoon dark corn syrup
- 3 medium eggs
- 2 cups white whole wheat flour
- 1/4 to 1 teaspoon salt, to taste
- 1 1/2 teaspoons active dry yeast
- 1/3 cup dried cherries

LARGE
- 3/4 cup milk, whole or skim
- 1/4 cup unsalted butter (or canola oil)
- 2 tablespoons dark corn syrup
- 3 medium eggs
- 3 1/2 cups white whole-wheat flour
- 1/2 to 1 1/2 teaspoons salt, to taste
- 2 teaspoons active dry yeast
- 1/2 cup dried cherries

Pour the milk into your baking pan and add the butter (or canola oil), unless the directions for your model instruct you to place the leavening in the very bottom of the pan first, the other dry ingredients next, and the liquids last. If you are making a large loaf and using butter straight from the refrigerator, cut the butter into chunks before placing it in the pan, since otherwise, being cold and hard, it will fail to blend evenly with the other ingredients. Spoon in the corn syrup and break the eggs into the pan. Add the flour, salt, and yeast, placing the yeast in its own separate dispenser if your machine has one.

Set the machine to its rapid-bake cycle for this loaf, and after the first kneading cycle or when the machine beeps its last call for ingredients, if yours does that, add the cherries.

This is a great loaf for leisurely brunches. It also makes a marvelous dessert sliced or cubed fresh from the oven and served in individual portions with a scoop of cherry vanilla ice cream, almost hidden beneath a slathering of walnuts in syrup and a dollop of whipped cream. Oh, yes, and, above everything — why not? — a bright big maraschino cherry.

Banana Chocolate Loaf

Real Honest-to-Goodness Hot Fudge Sauce

The flavors of banana and chocolate have a natural affinity for each other that is nowhere more evident than in this loaf, beneath whose unassuming pumpernickel-colored crust lies astonishing flavor. It owes its success to dried bananas, whose concentrated essence seems made for the bread machine bakery.

Dried bananas are now available in small, compressed packages in the exotic or tropical fruit section of many supermarkets. They last well, and you can have a couple of packs at the ready for when the sweet tooth strikes, without having to worry about the fruit turning black, as the fresh variety does all too soon.

SMALL	LARGE
¾ cup milk, whole or skim	1 cup milk
2 tablespoons unsalted butter	3 tablespoons unsalted butter
1 medium egg	1 medium egg
⅓ cup chopped pecans	½ cup chopped pecans
⅓ cup chopped dried bananas	½ cup chopped dried bananas
2¼ cups unbleached all-purpose flour	3 cups unbleached all-purpose flour
⅓ cup sugar	½ cup sugar
⅓ cup cocoa	½ cup cocoa
¼ to 1 teaspoon salt, to taste	½ to 1½ teaspoons salt, to taste
1½ teaspoons active dry yeast	2 teaspoons active dry yeast

Pour the milk into your bread machine baking pan and add the butter, egg, pecans, bananas, flour, sugar, cocoa, and salt. If your machine has a separate dispenser for leavening, spoon the yeast in there. Otherwise, scatter it over the rest of the ingredients in the pan, unless the instructions for the machine you have specify that it is to be placed in the very bottom of the pan first thing, in which case the other dry ingredients should be added next, the liquids last.

Bake the loaf on your machine's quick cycle.

Now here's the ultimate gooey Perrie's Delight. Slice a Banana Chocolate Loaf into individual servings while it's still warm. Mound vanilla ice cream on each slice, cover it with hot fudge sauce — the old-fashioned, preferably homemade, kind that hardens on the cold ice cream, as in the recipe below — and spoon over it some of those wonderful walnuts that come packed in syrup.

Then again, if that sounds too rich, Banana Chocolate Loaf is great simply sliced and served with butter.

REAL HONEST-TO-GOODNESS HOT FUDGE SAUCE

4 one-ounce squares unsweetened
   baking chocolate
3 tablespoons unsalted butter
⅔ cup water
1¾ cups sugar
¼ cup dark corn syrup
1 teaspoon vanilla extract

Melt the chocolate and butter in a heavy saucepan over very low heat. In a separate small pan, bring the water to a boil, then add it slowly to the chocolate-butter mixture, stirring constantly. Stir in the sugar and corn syrup and bring the sauce to a boil. Let it bubble, but not boil up, in the pan — and don't stir — for exactly 8 minutes. Remove it from the heat and add the vanilla extract, stirring until well blended.

Contrary to its name, hot fudge sauce is best served warm, not piping hot from the stove. It can be refrigerated and reheated, but in our house it's never, ever around long enough for that.

Peanut Butter–Chocolate Chip Loaf

Quick Chocolate-Candy-Bar Sauce

The favored flavors of the United States are epitomized in chocolate chips and peanut butter, here combined in a single loaf. I find the peanut butter a bit overwhelming myself, but Revell and his friends like ice cream and chocolate sauce sandwiches made with slices of the loaf.

Keep some chocolate chips in the freezer for this one. Freezing the chips isn't mandatory; the flavor of the loaf will be fine if you simply add room-temperature morsels in the normal course of events. But they'll be mushed by the bread machine's kneading blade, and then you won't bite into those dark, still-melted beads of chocolate that are such a treat when the loaf is still warm from the oven — which brings to mind grilled peanut butter sandwiches. Remember those? This bread is wonderful for them. The bits of chocolate melt all over again!

As any kid with braces can tell you, peanut butter varies a lot in consistency, from a spread as soft as yogurt to one firm enough to cement pieces of bread together. Should the product of your baking efforts be still uncooked in the center when you cut it open, reduce the liquid in the recipe by a few tablespoonfuls next time if you're still on the same jar of peanut butter.

Another thing to consider, if the peanut butter in your house is of the salted variety — ours isn't, so that's what I used in the recipe — be sparing in the measure of salt you use.

SMALL

1¼ *cups milk, whole or skim*

⅓ *cup peanut butter, creamy or*
   chunky

3 *tablespoons dark brown sugar*

2 *cups unbleached all-purpose flour*

¼ *cup wheat germ*

¼ to 1 teaspoon salt, to taste, de-
  pending especially on seasoning
  of peanut butter
1½ teaspoons active dry yeast
¾ cup frozen chocolate chips

Pour the milk into your bread machine baking pan and scoop in the peanut butter, unless the instructions that came with your machine call for placing the yeast in the bottom of the pan and reserving the liquids till last. Add the brown sugar, flour, wheat germ, and salt. If your machine features a separate dispenser for leavening, add the yeast there; otherwise, scatter it over the rest of the ingredients in the pan.

Set the machine to its rapid-bake cycle, and if your machine has a separate control for bread color, set it to light, since on the regular color setting the crust will be quite dark, although still acceptably so. Remember to toss in the frozen chocolate chips when the machine beeps its readiness to accept such whole entities. Failing that, add the chips when the first kneading cycle has been completed.

While the bread is still warm and the chocolate chips still gooey and the peanut butter still fragrant, cut the crusts from the loaf, slice it, and spread slightly softened vanilla ice cream and Quick Chocolate-Candy-Bar Sauce (see below) between pairs of slices. Serve to hungry after-schoolers.

QUICK CHOCOLATE-CANDY-BAR SAUCE

1¼ cups milk, whole or skim
1 five-ounce milk chocolate candy
  bar
1 teaspoon sugar
4 lightly beaten egg yolks
½ teaspoon vanilla extract

Place the milk, candy bar, and sugar in a heavy saucepan over low heat or in the top of a double boiler and stir constantly until the chocolate and sugar are melted. Remove from the heat and add the egg yolks in a slow stream, beating briskly. Return the pan to the stove and stir for 2 or 3 minutes longer or until the sauce thickens. Remove from the heat again and add the vanilla extract. Blend until smooth and creamy.

Raspberry Cream Loaf

Raspberry Melba Sauce

Fruit flavors are my favorites, although being asked to decide which one I like best of all would present a tough choice. I know that the rare durian, that queen of fruits prized above all others in the Orient, is not it. Fantasies and tales of the durian's fabulous taste once had Susan and me traipsing all over the hills of Sarawak, in Borneo, in search of this legendary delight. When we finally found some to sample, it tasted overwhelmingly of garlic butter gone rancid. Its pungent smell permeated the entire village, which was apparently celebrating its harvest with gustatory fervor, overcoming the olfactory glands.

No, my favorite fruit flavor would be something more traditional to the Western world. Either raspberry or strawberry would be it. Here's a raspberry winner.

SMALL
3/4 *cup sour cream or yogurt, regular or low-fat*
2 *tablespoons unsalted butter (or canola oil)*
1 1/2 *teaspoons raspberry extract*
1/3 *cup canned raspberry filling*
2 *cups unbleached all-purpose flour*
1/2 *cup wheat germ*

¼ to 1 teaspoon salt, to taste
1½ teaspoons active dry yeast

If the instructions that came with your bread machine call for the yeast to be placed in the baking pan first thing, remember to add the other dry ingredients before the liquids. Otherwise, scoop the sour cream or yogurt into your pan and add the butter (or canola oil), raspberry extract, raspberry filling, flour, wheat germ, and salt. Scatter the yeast over the top of the other ingredients or place it in its own separate dispenser if your machine has such a device.

Set the machine to its rapid-bake cycle for this loaf.

Once the loaf has cooled enough so that it can be sliced without difficulty, remove the top and bottom crusts and cut the remaining square or round into slices 1 to 1½ inches thick.

Serve the slices warm with a scoop of raspberry sorbet, a ladling of raspberry syrup or the Raspberry Melba Sauce below, and a few fresh raspberries scattered on top of it all. Talk about fruit flavor!

RASPBERRY MELBA SAUCE

⅓ cup red currant jelly
1 ten-ounce package frozen raspber-
  ries in syrup
1 teaspoon lemon juice
2 teaspoons water
1 tablespoon cornstarch

In a heavy saucepan set over low heat or in the top of a double boiler, melt the currant jelly. Add and stir the raspberries until thawed and bubbly. In a separate small bowl, mix the lemon juice and water and stir in the cornstarch to form a smooth paste. Blend this mixture into the berries. Bring the sauce to a boil, stirring constantly, and boil for 1 minute or until thickened.

This sauce is delectable either poured warm over a sorbet or served chilled, especially if there are a few fresh berries available to stir into the syrup just before serving.

Piña Colada Loaf

Polvo de Amor

The flavor of piña colada can be overwhelming. In this sweet, nutty-textured loaf, however, it is subtle, provoking one of those "Gee, it's great, reminds me of something" experiences we have when a taste is familiar but elusive, so that we can almost, but not quite, identify it.

The bits of coconut that get toasted into the crust as the loaf bakes are real taste treats, and they give you some idea of how good *Polvo de Amor*, or toasted coconut cream (see the recipe following the one for the loaf), is as an accompaniment.

You'll find the piña colada mix called for in the recipe among the beverage mixes at your supermarket.

SMALL	LARGE
1 cup piña colada mix	*1½ cups piña colada mix*
¼ cup canola or other light oil	*⅓ cup canola or other light oil*
½ cup firmly packed shredded coconut	*¾ cup firmly packed shredded coconut*
½ cup pecan halves	*⅔ cup pecan halves*
2½ cups unbleached all-purpose flour	*3½ cups unbleached all-purpose flour*
½ to 1 teaspoon salt, to taste	*1 to 2 teaspoons salt, to taste*
1½ teaspoons active dry yeast	*2 teaspoons active dry yeast*

Pour the piña colada mix and oil into your baking pan and add the coconut, pecans, flour, salt, and yeast. Be sure to follow the directions that came with your particular machine for incorporating the leavening, since the instructions for some models specify reversing the order in which the ingredients are placed in the pan.

To bake the loaf, set the machine to its quick cycle.

A Piña Colada Loaf lends itself to a sweet molasses glaze made by beating together 1 tablespoon unsulfured molasses and 1 tablespoon of hot water. The glaze can be brushed over the crown of the loaf when it emerges from the electronic oven and, for super visual appeal, dusted with toasted shredded coconut, which adheres well to the sticky glaze. To brown this extra coconut, spread the strands out on a cookie sheet and bake them in an oven preheated to 350 degrees F. for about 10 minutes.

Another attractive presentation for the loaf is à la mode, with a simply made but delectable topping called *Polvo de Amor* in Spanish. The coconut cream called for in the recipe is found canned in the Latin American section of many grocery stores.

POLVO DE AMOR

1 cup canned coconut cream
3 tablespoons sugar

Pour the coconut cream into a small saucepan and add the sugar. Stir and cook over low heat until the mixture browns attractively.

To serve, lay generous individual slices of the Piña Colada Loaf on dessert plates, put a scoop of vanilla ice cream on each, and top with the *Polvo de Amor* as you would with a hot fudge sauce. For true coconut enthusiasts.

Peach Praline Loaf

Creamy Caramel Sauce

Here's a simple, quickly made loaf that originated because my daughter Tanya so often left half a canful of peaches in the refrigerator after making a snack of the rest. The canned fruit adds more softness and tenderness than actual taste to the finished product. However, while the flavor is mild, slices of the loaf, particularly when toasted, make a great base on which to float a large scoop of peach ice cream or frozen yogurt covered by Creamy Caramel Sauce (see the recipe following the one for the loaf).

The canned peaches to be found in our refrigerator, and hence in this loaf, are of the no-sugar-added variety.

If your machine has difficulty with this dough, which is very dry until the moisture is extracted from the peaches by the machine's kneading action, liquefy the peaches in a blender before adding them to the baking pan.

SMALL	LARGE
1 cup canned sliced unsweetened peaches, with liquid	1½ cups canned sliced unsweetened peaches, with liquid
1 teaspoon unsalted butter (or canola oil)	2 teaspoons unsalted butter (or canola oil)
1 medium egg	1 medium egg
½ teaspoon vanilla extract	1 teaspoon vanilla extract
¼ teaspoon almond extract	½ teaspoon almond extract
½ cup pecan halves	¾ cup pecan halves
2 cups unbleached all-purpose flour	3 cups unbleached all-purpose flour
½ cup semolina flour	¾ cup semolina flour
¼ to 1 teaspoon salt, to taste	½ to 1½ teaspoons salt, to taste
1½ teaspoons active dry yeast	2 teaspoons active dry yeast

Place the peaches together with their canning liquid in the baking pan of your bread machine, unless the instructions that came with your machine specify that the yeast is to be placed first in the bottom of the pan, followed by the other dry ingredients and, last, the liquids. Add the butter (or canola oil), egg, vanilla and almond extracts, pecans, all-purpose and semolina flours, salt, and yeast. If your machine has a separate dispenser for leavening, spoon the yeast in there; otherwise, scatter it over the rest of the ingredients.

Use the machine's rapid-bake cycle for this loaf.

While a peach praline dessert can certainly be concocted with a ready-made topping, no commercial variety can match the following simple homemade caramel sauce for this dessert.

CREAMY CARAMEL SAUCE

2 cups sugar
2 cups heavy cream, heated
1 teaspoon vanilla extract

Place the sugar in a large heavy saucepan or skillet set over very low heat and stir it with a long-handled wooden spoon just until melted. It will lump as it melts. Not to worry. Remove it from the heat and carefully, keeping your distance (since the next step may result in some sizzle and steam), add the heated cream a little at a time, stirring constantly. Return the pan to the heat and cook the sauce, stirring slowly, until it is smooth and syrupy. Remove from the heat and blend in the vanilla extract. Serve immediately.

Yet Another Chocolate Loaf

Chocolate Buttercream Filling
Satin Chocolate Glaze

Can one have too much chocolate? Not according to Tanya and Revell. Perhaps for that reason, I couldn't resist adding one more recipe for a chocolate loaf as a grand finale to this chapter. Especially when I discovered that this one — which has a rich, dense, fudgy texture, although not the sweetness of true fudge — is wonderfully and wickedly complemented by Chocolate Buttercream Filling, Satin Chocolate Glaze (see the recipes following the one for the loaf), and ice cream over all. The contrast of the satin glaze with the soft ice cream is marvelous.

A greater quantity of dough than that of the recipe below is more than a bread machine can handle. Let that not deter you from making the so-called small loaf.

SMALL
½ cup buttermilk
⅓ cup milk, whole or skim
1 medium egg
1 teaspoon chocolate extract
½ teaspoon vanilla extract
1 cup unbleached all-purpose flour

¹/₃ cup barley flour
¹/₄ cup semolina flour
¹/₄ cup millet flour
¹/₄ cup graham cracker crumbs
¹/₄ cup cocoa
¹/₃ cup sugar
1 tablespoon instant coffee, regular
  or decaffeinated
¹/₄ to 1 teaspoon salt, to taste
2 teaspoons active dry yeast

Unless the instructions for your particular bread machine specify that the yeast is to be placed in the bottom of the pan first thing, followed by the other dry ingredients and then the liquids, pour the buttermilk and milk into your baking pan. Break the egg into the pan and add the chocolate and vanilla extracts, followed by the all-purpose, barley, semolina, and millet flours. Measure in the graham cracker crumbs, cocoa, sugar, instant coffee, salt, and yeast, placing the leavening in its own separate dispenser if your machine has that feature.

Bake the loaf on the machine's quick cycle.

Because it is rich but not sugary, this cake can be lavishly spread with buttercream without becoming a too cloyingly sweet confection. Buttercream can be used to ice the top of the loaf as well, but it is lovely with the deep, dark Satin Chocolate Glaze, especially if servings are to be topped with ice cream.

CHOCOLATE BUTTERCREAM FILLING

3 tablespoons unsalted butter
1 cup confectioners' sugar
¹/₃ cup cocoa
1 tablespoon dark corn syrup
2 tablespoons heavy cream
¹/₂ teaspoon vanilla extract

Cream the butter in a small bowl. Mix the confectioners' sugar and cocoa together and blend them into the butter a little at a time. Stir in the corn syrup, cream, and vanilla extract, and beat the mixture at high speed for 2 to 3 minutes or until the buttercream is of a good spreading consistency.

Cut the top and bottom crusts from the chocolate loaf, slice it crosswise to make layers, and fill with the buttercream. Content yourself with a buttercream topping as well, or take just a few minutes to create the following handsome glossy glaze for the cake.

SATIN CHOCOLATE GLAZE

2 tablespoons sugar
2 tablespoons water
½ cup semisweet chocolate chips

In a small saucepan, bring the sugar and water to a boil, stirring until the sugar is completely dissolved. Melt the chocolate chips into the mix, remove from the heat, and stir until the icing is fairly stiff but still spreadable. It will harden to a smooth, satiny glaze.

Slices of this treat served à la mode need no further enrichment.

6 · Sauced and Soused Loaves

A DESSERT DRENCHED in a sauce has about it a certain down-home quality associated in many people's minds with the treat looked forward to as children all through the obligatory dinner preceding it. The simple cake or square of some other floury delicacy filled up those corners left hungry by the mandatory forkful of the vegetable of the day, and the sauce, frequently a warm one — and certainly a sweet one — was oh so satisfying. Thus, such desserts often have great comfort appeal.

Despite the homely inspiration for such desserts, the offerings in this chapter are by no means plain and simple. The choice of possible embellishments is nearly endless, and the yield from your bread machine bakery with a sauce or a mousse filling can be quite elegant, as witness the nobly domed *Zuccotto* (see page 92). So let your imagination, and perhaps memories, play with the desserts in this chapter.

Lemon Suzette Loaf

Suzette Sauce

Citrus oils are quite volatile, and their flavor often vanishes during prolonged cooking. This is why breads calling for citrus zest or citrus oil are so often baking-powder loaves, whose cooking time is normally shorter than that of yeast breads. Since the bread machines on the market as yet have no really short cycle to accommodate these quick breads, however, I've had to work around that limitation.

Here's a yeast-based loaf formulated especially for bread machines that's very nearly a cake and certainly lemony. Serve slices of it flooded with warm Suzette Sauce (see the recipe below the one for the loaf) — yes, it's the sauce of crepes, but it can be so much more! — with or without a layer of vanilla ice cream or lemon sherbet in between.

SMALL	LARGE
1 cup milk, whole or skim	1 1/4 cups milk, whole or skim
3 tablespoons unsalted butter (or canola oil)	1/4 cup unsalted butter (or canola oil)
1 tablespoon lemon juice	1 tablespoon + 2 teaspoons lemon juice
grated zest of 1 small lemon	grated zest of 1 large or 2 small lemons
1 1/2 cups semolina flour	2 cups semolina flour
1 cup unbleached all-purpose flour	1 1/3 cups unbleached all-purpose flour
1/2 cup sugar	2/3 cup sugar
1/4 to 1 teaspoon salt, to taste	1/2 to 1 1/2 teaspoons salt, to taste
1 1/2 teaspoons active dry yeast	2 teaspoons active dry yeast

Pour the milk into the baking pan of your bread machine and add the butter (or canola oil), lemon juice, lemon zest, semolina and all-purpose flours, sugar, salt, and yeast, placing the leavening in its own separate dispenser if your machine has one. Remember, however, that if the instructions accompanying your model call for placing the leavening in the bottom of the pan first thing, then the other dry ingredients should be added next, before the liquids.

Bake the loaf on your machine's quick cycle.

SUZETTE SAUCE

> ½ cup (1 stick) unsalted butter
> ½ cup sugar
> 2 tablespoons orange juice
> 2 to 3 teaspoons grated orange zest,
>   to taste

Melt the butter in a small heavy saucepan and stir in the sugar. Add the orange juice and orange zest and bring the mixture to a boil. Lower the heat and simmer for 2 minutes. Pour into a warmed pitcher and let everyone help themselves.

Currant Ginger Loaf

Hard Sauce

Here's a loaf my father would have loved. Ginger was one of his favorite spices, and, as Susan put it, "This one's for people who really like ginger." If the gingerroot you procure happens to be very fresh and the flavor promises to be too strong to suit your taste, reduce the amount of ginger called for in the recipe.

The currants found among the ingredients for this loaf lend it contrast in both taste and texture when they're kept whole. This can be achieved by reserving them to toss into the baking pan when the machine beeps, if it's the type of machine that does that, or after the first kneading cycle, if your machine is the strong, silent type.

For a real treat, serve warm slices of this bread with homemade rum- or brandy-flavored Hard Sauce (see the recipe following the one for the loaf).

(see the recipe following the one for the loaf)

SMALL	LARGE
½ cup buttermilk	*¾ cup buttermilk*
2 tablespoons unsalted butter (or canola oil)	*3 tablespoons unsalted butter (or canola oil)*
1 medium egg	*1 large egg*
2 tablespoons thinly sliced peeled fresh ginger	*3 tablespoons thinly sliced peeled fresh ginger*
2 teaspoons lemon juice	*1 tablespoon lemon juice*
2 cups unbleached all-purpose flour	*3 cups unbleached all-purpose flour*
¼ cup uncooked oatmeal (not instant)	*⅓ cup uncooked oatmeal (not instant)*
2 tablespoons dark brown sugar	*3 tablespoons dark brown sugar*
¼ to 1 teaspoon salt, to taste	*½ to 1½ teaspoons salt, to taste*
1½ teaspoons active dry yeast	*2 teaspoons active dry yeast*
½ cup dried currants	*¾ cup dried currants*

Unless the instructions for your bread machine specify that the yeast is to be placed in the bottom of the baking pan, followed by the other dry ingredients and then the liquids, measure the buttermilk into your pan and add the butter (or canola oil), egg, ginger, lemon juice, flour, oatmeal, brown sugar, salt, and yeast, placing the leavening in its own separate dispenser if your machine has that feature.

Set the machine to its rapid-bake cycle and let it start churning away. At the beep or, failing that, after the first kneading cycle, add the currants. If you're planning on the homemade Hard Sauce below as an accompaniment to this loaf, you might want to whip it up while you're waiting for the beep, so it can be chilling while the bread bakes.

HARD SAUCE

½ cup (1 stick) unsalted butter, softened

¾ cup confectioners' sugar
1 to 2 tablespoons rum or brandy
or your own favorite liqueur

In a small bowl, cream the butter until smooth. Slowly add the confectioners' sugar and beat until fluffy. Blend in the rum, brandy, or other liqueur.

While the Hard Sauce can be served simply chilled in a small bowl and perhaps garnished with a few sprigs of mint, for a pretty display it can also be piped into individual rosettes, using a pastry tube or a cookie press fitted with a star tip. Pipe the rosettes onto a foil-lined cookie sheet or tray, freeze them uncovered until hard, transfer them to a regular freezer container, and you'll have decorative rosettes ready anytime you need them.

Pudding Bread

Lemon Sauce

At the conclusion of a dinner we were having at the home of some friends in London, their daughter Lucy, on seeing the ice cream for dessert, exclaimed, "Oh, my favorite pudding!"

Our own daughter, Tanya, looked rather nonplussed. "But that's not pudding, is it? It's ice cream."

"Well, yes, we're having ice cream for pudding."

The word "pudding" was bandied about with considerable mirth until we colonials finally understood that what we call dessert the English call pudding — whether it is or not.

Well, here's a pudding that's actually bread, or vice versa. Hard sauce is the traditional accompaniment to a pudding; see the recipe

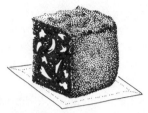

immediately preceding, which is presented as a topping for the Currant Ginger Loaf. Served with this sauce or Lemon Sauce (see the recipe below the one for the Pudding Bread), it's a fine winter dessert. Buttered like scones, it belongs in front of a crackling fire with some tea. In either case, it's substantial fare, as you might surmise from the absence of a recipe for a large loaf. There are big chunks of apricots and nuts in every rich, rough-textured bite.

SMALL

1 cup sour cream or yogurt, regular or low-fat

½ cup apple cider

¼ cup unsulfured molasses

1 medium egg

½ cup dried apricots

½ cup dried apples

½ cup hazelnuts

½ cup pecan halves

1½ cups wheat bran

¾ cup unbleached all-purpose flour

½ cup cornmeal

½ to 1 teaspoon salt, to taste

2 teaspoons active dry yeast

Scoop the sour cream or yogurt into the baking pan of your bread machine and add the cider and molasses, unless the instructions for your particular machine specify that the leavening is to be placed in the pan first and the liquids last. Break the egg into the pan, then measure in the apricots, apples, hazelnuts, pecans, wheat bran, flour, cornmeal, and salt. Distribute the yeast according to the instructions for your machine.

Bake on the machine's quick cycle.

For a lovely piquant accent to this pudding, try the following sunny Lemon Sauce.

LEMON SAUCE

1 tablespoon cornstarch
1 cup water
6 tablespoons lemon juice
½ cup sugar
grated zest of 1 medium lemon

Place the cornstarch in a small bowl and gradually stir in ¼ cup of the water, pouring the rest into a small saucepan or the top of a double boiler. Blend the cornstarch solution until smooth. To the water in the saucepan add the lemon juice and sugar. Heat these ingredients, stirring until the sugar is completely dissolved. Then blend the cornstarch solution into the lemon mixture and simmer, stirring constantly, until the sauce is thick and clear. Add the lemon zest and transfer the hot sauce to an attractive small pitcher from which it can be poured over individual helpings of the Pudding Bread as desired.

Pear Loaf

Cherry Sauce

Pears are one of the few fruits that ripen well off the tree. Stone fruits, such as peaches and plums, harvested early never seem to attain the sweet, redolent flavor of those picked by hand in the dappled shade of the orchard at the very moment they are about to drop. In fact, it's not unusual for a store-bought plum to go from rock to rot without much flavor in between.

Pears are different. They actually ripen better off a tree than on it. They also dry exceedingly well, and in their dried form they add a very pleasant tangy flavor to a loaf. Try serving slices of this one fresh from the electronic oven with a simple, warm, sweet Cherry Sauce (see the recipe following the one for the loaf).

SMALL
3/4 cup yogurt, regular or low-fat
3 tablespoons unsalted butter (or
  canola oil)
2 tablespoons honey
3/4 cup dried pears
2 1/4 cups unbleached all-purpose
  flour
1/2 to 1 teaspoon salt, to taste
1 1/2 teaspoons active dry yeast

Spoon the yogurt into your bread machine baking pan and add the butter (or canola oil), honey, pears, flour, salt, and yeast, placing the leavening in its own separate dispenser if your machine has one. Where the instructions for your particular machine call for placing the yeast in the bottom of the pan first thing, remember to reverse the order in which you add the liquids and the other dry ingredients.

Set the machine to its rapid-bake cycle for this loaf.

Pear Loaf

Cherry Sauce

Pears are one of the few fruits that ripen well off the tree. Stone fruits, such as peaches and plums, harvested early never seem to attain the sweet, redolent flavor of those picked by hand in the dappled shade of the orchard at the very moment they are about to drop. In fact, it's not unusual for a store-bought plum to go from rock to rot without much flavor in between.

Pears are different. They actually ripen better off a tree than on it. They also dry exceedingly well, and in their dried form they add a very pleasant tangy flavor to a loaf. Try serving slices of this one fresh from the electronic oven with a simple, warm, sweet Cherry Sauce (see the recipe following the one for the loaf).

SMALL

¾ cup yogurt, regular or low-fat

3 tablespoons unsalted butter (or canola oil)

2 tablespoons honey

¾ cup dried pears

2¼ cups unbleached all-purpose flour

½ to 1 teaspoon salt, to taste

1½ teaspoons active dry yeast

Spoon the yogurt into your bread machine baking pan and add the butter (or canola oil), honey, pears, flour, salt, and yeast, placing the leavening in its own separate dispenser if your machine has one. Where the instructions for your particular machine call for placing the yeast in the bottom of the pan first thing, remember to reverse the order in which you add the liquids and the other dry ingredients.

Set the machine to its rapid-bake cycle for this loaf.

cornmeal, and salt. Distribute the yeast according to the instructions for your machine.

Bake on the machine's quick cycle.

For a lovely piquant accent to this pudding, try the following sunny Lemon Sauce.

LEMON SAUCE

> *1 tablespoon cornstarch*
> *1 cup water*
> *6 tablespoons lemon juice*
> *½ cup sugar*
> *grated zest of 1 medium lemon*

Place the cornstarch in a small bowl and gradually stir in ¼ cup of the water, pouring the rest into a small saucepan or the top of a double boiler. Blend the cornstarch solution until smooth. To the water in the saucepan add the lemon juice and sugar. Heat these ingredients, stirring until the sugar is completely dissolved. Then blend the cornstarch solution into the lemon mixture and simmer, stirring constantly, until the sauce is thick and clear. Add the lemon zest and transfer the hot sauce to an attractive small pitcher from which it can be poured over individual helpings of the Pudding Bread as desired.

to cool the contents just a bit, and transfer the cherries to your food processor or blender. Puree them until they are very smooth.

Return the puree to the saucepan, add the sugar, and cook for another minute. Pour the corn syrup into a measuring cup, add the cornstarch, and blend this mixture to a smooth paste. Stir the paste into the sauce and simmer very slowly, stirring constantly, until the sauce is dark and thick. Serve hot and fragrant.

Crunchy Caramel Apple-Granola Loaf

Butterscotch Sauce Pure and Simple

One of the toughest choices facing our kids every August and September was whether to have the caramel-covered apples or the red sugar-coated ones at the Woodstock and Brooklyn fairs. The cotton candy was easily chosen — always red, never blue, always on a paper cone, never in a bag. Ah, life's choices should always remain so clear-cut.

For me the choice in apples was simple. The caramel-covered ones didn't stick to the teeth. The same holds true for this easy-to-make treat.

To serve with a cherry sauce, first remove the crusts of your Pear Loaf. If you make the cut for the crusts about 1 inch in from the sides and freeze these edges, they will enhance your next chocolate fondue wonderfully. The flavors of pear and chocolate are glorious together.

Slice the remaining loaf into 1-inch-thick pieces. Pour some cherry sauce onto individual dessert dishes and place a slice of Pear Loaf in the sauce on each plate. Grace the top with a liberal dollop of whipped cream and decorate with grated chocolate or, for a really pretty effect, a generous sprinkling of chocolate curls.

The sauce for this dessert can be a commercial one or simply the contents of a can of tart red cherry pie filling heated in a saucepan over medium heat. But for a memorable treat, try the homemade sauce with dried cherries given below. Since you don't have to pit them, stirring up this sauce takes next to no time, and it's truly luscious.

CHERRY SAUCE

> *1 cup dried cherries*
> *1½ cups water*
> *¼ cup sugar*
> *¼ cup dark corn syrup*
> *1 tablespoon cornstarch*

Place the cherries in a heavy saucepan, cover them with 1¼ cups of the water, and bring the mixture to a simmer over very low heat. Continue to simmer for 5 minutes or until the cherries are plump and tender.

Remove the pan from the heat, add the remaining ¼ cup of water

SMALL	LARGE
1 cup sour cream or yogurt, regular or low-fat	*1⅓ cups sour cream or yogurt, regular or low-fat*
1 tablespoon unsalted butter or canola oil	*2 tablespoons unsalted butter or canola oil*
½ cup honey	*⅔ cup honey*
1 medium egg	*1 medium egg*
1 small unpeeled but cored apple, diced	*1 large unpeeled but cored apple, diced*
1¾ cups unbleached all-purpose flour	*3 cups unbleached all-purpose flour*
1 cup granola	*1½ cups granola*
1 teaspoon ground nutmeg	*1½ teaspoons ground nutmeg*
¼ to 1 teaspoon salt, to taste	*½ to 1½ teaspoons salt, to taste*
1½ teaspoons active dry yeast	*2 teaspoons active dry yeast*

Unless the instructions that came with your bread machine call for starting with the leavening, scoop the sour cream or yogurt into your baking pan and add the butter or canola oil, honey, egg, apple, flour, granola, nutmeg, and salt. If your machine has a separate dispenser for the yeast, measure it in there. If not, scatter it over the other dry ingredients.

Set your machine to its rapid-bake cycle for this loaf.

The dough will be quite stiff. So if you're not dashing out the door, check the bread pan 5 or 10 minutes into the kneading cycle, especially if you are making the big loaf in an oblong pan, to be sure the machine is collecting all the ingredients from the corners of the pan. If it's not, scrape the sides down once, using a rubber spatula, to make sure everything is incorporated into the dough.

For a lovely dessert, once the loaf is baked and cooled, cut off the top and bottom crusts along with about 1 inch of the inner crumb. Freeze these slices for later use with a fondue or in a bread pudding.

Cut the remaining loaf into 1-inch-thick slices, place them on individual serving plates, and cover them with a good butterscotch sauce, store-bought or homemade (see below). Top that with whipped cream for extra opulence and sprinkle a little extra crunchy granola over all.

BUTTERSCOTCH SAUCE PURE AND SIMPLE

½ cup (1 stick) unsalted butter
1 cup dark corn syrup
2 cups dark brown sugar
½ cup heavy cream
1 teaspoon vanilla extract

Melt the butter in a heavy saucepan over low heat. Add the corn syrup and then, gradually, the brown sugar, stirring until blended. Bring the mixture to a boil, reduce the heat, and simmer, stirring constantly, for 3 to 5 minutes or until the sauce is the consistency of heavy syrup. Remove from the heat and blend in the cream and vanilla extract. The aroma of this sauce is heavenly.

Figs and Cream Loaf

Prune Sauce

Here's a dark, rich, substantial confection in the tradition of English holiday desserts that will have you thinking of Dickens. A compact cake with a muffin-y crust, it's wonderful sliced thin and spread with sweet butter for tea. For a company dinner, serve ample squares of it with the thick, syrupy Prune Sauce that follows the cake recipe.

SMALL	LARGE
1 cup heavy cream	1½ cups heavy cream
2 tablespoons unsalted butter (or canola oil)	3 tablespoons unsalted butter (or canola oil)
2 tablespoons honey	3 tablespoons honey
½ cup dried figs, stems removed, quartered	¾ cup dried figs, stems removed, quartered

1 cup unbleached all-purpose flour	1½ cups unbleached all-purpose flour
1 cup whole wheat flour	1½ cups whole wheat flour
¼ teaspoon ground cloves	½ teaspoon ground cloves
¼ teaspoon ground allspice	½ teaspoon ground allspice
½ to 1 teaspoon salt, to taste	1 to 2 teaspoons salt, to taste
1½ teaspoons active dry yeast	2 teaspoons active dry yeast

Remember that if the instructions accompanying your bread machine call for the yeast to be placed in the baking pan first, the dry ingredients should be added before the liquids. Otherwise, pour the cream into your pan and add the butter (or canola oil), honey, figs, all-purpose and whole wheat flours, cloves, allspice, salt, and yeast. If your machine has a separate dispenser for leavening, spoon the yeast in there after all the other ingredients have been measured into the baking pan.

Set your machine to its quick setting for this loaf.

The following dark, velvety Prune Sauce complements a Figs and Cream cake superbly. Neither the cake nor the sauce is cloyingly sweet, although the latter is rich and full-bodied, and together they provide a surprisingly healthy dose of fiber, vitamins, and minerals — in all honesty, not an unhealthful dessert.

PRUNE SAUCE

1 cup pitted prunes, firmly packed
water to cover
2 tablespoons lemon juice
1 tablespoon grated orange zest
½ teaspoon ground cloves
¼ teaspoon ground nutmeg
¼ teaspoon ground cinnamon
½ cup sugar
½ cup red wine or port

Place the prunes in a heavy saucepan, barely cover with water, and stir in the lemon juice, orange zest, cloves, nutmeg, and cinnamon. Bring the mixture to the boiling point, then lower the heat and gently simmer for 15 minutes or until the prunes are soft, stirring occasionally.

Transfer the mixture to the bowl of a food processor or a blender and puree until smooth.

Return the puree to the saucepan, add the sugar and wine or port, and continue to cook the sauce over low heat until it is velvety and hot.

Squares of the Figs and Cream cake are attractively served simply topped by a dollop of whipped cream, with the Prune Sauce as an accompaniment to be ladled over individual helpings as modestly or generously as desired.

Zuccotto

Zuccotto Filling
Zuccotto Frosting

The quintessentially Florentine *Zuccotto* is a showy centerpiece confection that's quickly assembled. It will want 4 to 6 hours of chilling in the refrigerator once it's put together, so that much advance planning is required. But this very fact is what makes it such a wonderful company dessert, for it's finished long before the guests arrive or you need to turn your attention to other dinner preparations.

A spectacular half-sphere of a cake completely enveloped in snowy whipped cream, the *Zuccotto* discloses its true nature only upon being sliced, for it is a filled cake whose creamy center comes in many different flavors. The recipe adapted here for the bread machine bakery uses a filling quickly and easily made, to go with the bread so effortlessly conjured up by your bread machine. One time-saver deserves another, after all.

The unique contour of *zuccotti* is traditionally achieved with the help of a special half-round mold suggesting a gourd or a pumpkin cut in two: hence the name *zuccotto*, or "little pumpkin." Doubtless the specialty bakers' catalogs in this country will soon carry such molds, but an ordinary 2½-quart glass or stainless steel mixing bowl works just fine for this dish.

Traditionally, the base for *zuccotti* is a sponge cake. Here a certain adjustment had to be made for the bread machine bakery, since bread machines can't make true sponge cakes. But loaves such as the Light Citrus, Banana Almond, and Lemon Suzette, whose recipes are found earlier in this volume, make very respectable shells for a *zuccotto*, even though not completely authentic renderings of the original.

If you haven't much of any of the loaves mentioned left among the slices tucked away in your freezer, you can use lots of tops and bottoms saved from other loaves, provided they aren't too strongly flavored in any one direction. And, of course, you can always toss the ingredients for, say, a fresh citrus loaf into your bread machine if you know a little in advance that you'll be wanting to serve this elegant dessert.

ZUCCOTTO FILLING

8 one-ounce squares semisweet baking chocolate
1¼ cups heavy cream, well chilled
1 tablespoon instant espresso
1 package (3⅜ ounces) vanilla
  pudding mix
1½ cups milk, whole or skim
1 teaspoon almond extract

almond liqueur (approximately ¼
  cup)

Coarsely grate 4 squares of the semisweet chocolate. (To save fingers, I grate just half of each square, working my way across it parallel to that convenient groove provided for cutting the block in half, and grating right up to the notch. To get the 4 ounces called for, I thus grate the first half, so to speak, of 8 squares of chocolate.) Set the grated chocolate aside for the moment.

In a small heavy saucepan over very low heat or in a glass bowl in the microwave, melt the other 4 ounces of the chocolate. Set this aside as well.

Pour the cream into a chilled mixing bowl and whip lightly. Add the instant espresso and continue beating until the cream forms stiff peaks.

In a separate bowl, combine the vanilla pudding mix with the milk and stir in the almond extract. Fold the grated chocolate and whipped cream into the pudding.

To assemble the *Zuccotto*, cut the loaf you plan to use into slices about ½ inch thick. If you're using leftover slices, it doesn't matter if they happen to be a little fatter or a little thinner than that. They should all be about the same thickness, though.

Stack the slices together and cut the stack in half diagonally so that you end up with 2 piles of triangles or, in the case of a round loaf, half-rounds. Separate the triangles or half-circles and sprinkle them with the almond liqueur.

Line your ersatz *Zuccotto* mold with plastic wrap. Reserving enough of the bread to cover the top of the bowl, wedge the remaining triangles or half-rounds snugly into the bowl, facing them all the same way so that their bottom points meet at the center and they

radiate out in a star pattern. What you're striving for is a compact concave shell. This concentrated endeavor leads to fairly fragrant hands. The first time I made a *Zuccotto* the kids commented on my new after-shave.

Line the inside of the shell you've created with about half the pudding mixture, keeping to the outside of the bowl in order to leave room at the center for the remainder of the pudding. Then fold the melted chocolate into the remaining half of the pudding and fill in the center of the shell with this darker mixture.

Now cover the top of the pudding with the reserved triangles or half-rounds. This top will be the bottom once you invert the bowl, which you will do to serve the dessert, so don't worry about the pieces fitting together perfectly. But trim their edges so they don't extend beyond the bowl.

Cover the bowl tightly with plastic wrap and refrigerate the *Zuccotto* for 4 to 6 hours. An overnight's resting doesn't hurt it at all. The serving plate you intend to use can be inverted over it to stay cold as well.

ZUCCOTTO FROSTING

3/4 cup heavy cream, well chilled
3 tablespoons confectioners' sugar
1 tablespoon instant espresso

blanched almonds, chopped and
toasted, for garnish

In a small chilled bowl, beat the cream lightly, add the confectioners' sugar and instant espresso, and continue to beat until the frosting is thick and fluffy.

Take the *Zuccotto* from the refrigerator, uncover and invert the bowl over the chilled serving plate, and unmold the cake. Carefully remove the plastic wrap around it and frost it with the whipped cream. Garnish the dome with golden toasted almonds.

7 · Twice-Baked Cookies

 OVEN-DRIED, OR TWICE-BAKED, rusks and cookies have a long culinary history in Europe. From the *biscotti* of Italy to the zwieback of Germany and the *skorpor* of Sweden, these traditional homely nibbles — many of them quite nutritional and low in fat for all their engaging flavor — are made from breads cut into oblong bars that are then baked a second time in a slow oven.

To add a little moisture and a touch of naughtiness to what is otherwise rather dry fare, *biscotti* are sometimes dipped in chocolate after the second baking. They've also been known to be dipped in a glass of the sweet Tuscan wine *vin santo*. Zwieback and *skorpor* are frequently softened by being dunked in the coffee, tea, or cocoa with which they are so often served.

Dunking isn't very proper, my mother was wont to point out. But she would indulge in it when having a little bite on her own, and, personally, I find dunking a good bread in a flavorsome beverage one of the true pleasures of life, marred only, on occasion, by a piece of the baked goods dropping off and splashing into the cup, with the inevitable result of a spotted shirt. Well, no one said dunking was neat. Perhaps that's why it tends to be a solitary endeavor. In any event, whether accompanied by an appropriate beverage or dunked in it, twice-baked cookies are a pleasure to nibble on.

Now thrice-baked fare — that might seem to be pushing it. But I feel compelled to add here that, ground to a crumb, *biscotti* and rusks make tasty pie shells when substituted for graham crackers in the crust of the same name.

Plain Rusks

Summer is a special time in the part of Sweden where I spent my childhood, the sunlit days seeming to last forever, the twilight lingering till nearly midnight. Some of my fondest memories of that time are of sitting on a large rock in the woods not far from our house on those sunny afternoons and white nights drinking *saft*, the Swedish drink of diluted fruit syrup, and eating *skorpor*, or simple rusks.

Susan's comment on first tasting these rusks was "Bland, aren't they! I can see why you'd be led to dunk them in something."

So, in the spirit of compromise, when I bake bread for rusks I now cut about 1 inch off the top and bottom of the loaf, sandwich a layer of sliced bananas between these two extremities, and cover the resulting flat cake with a melba sauce for a dessert everyone in the family likes. Then, from the center, I make plain rusks for myself.

SMALL

3/4 cup milk, whole or skim
2 tablespoons unsalted butter
1 tablespoon solid vegetable shortening
2 cups unbleached all-purpose flour
1/4 cup sugar
1/4 to 1 teaspoon salt, to taste
1 1/2 teaspoons active dry yeast

LARGE

1 1/4 cups milk, whole or skim
3 tablespoons unsalted butter
2 tablespoons solid vegetable shortening
3 1/2 cups unbleached all-purpose flour
1/3 cup sugar
1/2 to 1 1/2 teaspoons salt, to taste
2 teaspoons active dry yeast

Pour the milk into your bread machine baking pan and add the butter, shortening, flour, sugar, salt, and yeast, following the directions that came with your particular machine for incorporating the leavening, since some machines specify reversing the order in which the ingredients are placed in the pan.

Bake the loaf on your machine's quick cycle.

To make the rusks, cut the cooled loaf into slices approximately ¾ to 1 inch thick. Cut these slices in turn into bars 1 or 1¼ inches wide. Precision doesn't really count here. In fact, the rustic look of un-evenly sized pieces is a plus, adding a certain homeyness.

Place the bars on an ungreased cookie sheet and dry them in your regular oven at 350 degrees F. for 10 to 15 minutes or until golden brown, turning them once halfway through the baking time for more even toasting. Cool the rusks thoroughly on racks and store them tightly covered — if there are any left after you've sampled them.

Silver Birch Biscotti

Dipping Chocolate

Hippie remnants of the sixties are scattered throughout our con-temporary culture, from Doonesbury to the revival fashions of retro rock radio. Coffeehouses reminiscent of the beatnik era — my own, I object when the kids mistakenly put me in the Woodstock set — are mushrooming across the country. So finding recently in rural eastern Connecticut what in earlier years would have passed for a flower-power coffee-shop-cum-bakery came as no surprise to me, although its clientele, ranging from high-schoolers to senior citizens in their sixties and seventies, seemed oblivious to any Haight-Ashbury connection.

But times, and pastries, change. Eclairs have gone the way of the Devil Dog, displaced by the likes of *biscotti*, although they're often dipped in chocolate. The fare at the Silver Birch Bakery, as close to a Bleeker Street coffeehouse as I can find in our area, is no exception.

The California adaptation of Italian *biscotti*, on which this recipe is based, calls for pine nuts, but Carolyn Berke, proprietress of the Silver Birch Bakery, modified the recipe to bring back the more traditional European walnut. In adapting the recipe for bread machines, I added millet flour, to improve the texture, and yeast, because baking powder alone would not leaven the dough sufficiently.

SMALL	LARGE
1/2 cup orange juice	*3/4 cup orange juice*
2 tablespoons unsalted butter	*3 tablespoons unsalted butter*
1 tablespoon solid vegetable shortening	*2 tablespoons solid vegetable shortening*
1 medium egg	*2 medium eggs*
3/4 cup walnut halves	*1 cup walnut halves*
2 cups unbleached all-purpose flour	*3 cups unbleached all-purpose flour*
1/4 cup millet flour	*1/2 cup millet flour*
1/3 cup sugar	*1/2 cup sugar*
1/2 teaspoon ground ginger	*1 teaspoon ground ginger*
1/4 to 1 teaspoon salt, to taste	*1/2 to 1 1/2 teaspoons salt, to taste*
1 teaspoon double-acting baking powder	*2 teaspoons double-acting baking powder*
1 1/2 teaspoons active dry yeast	*2 teaspoons active dry yeast*

Pour the orange juice into the baking pan of your bread machine, add the butter and shortening, and break the egg or eggs, depending on the size of the loaf you are making, into the pan. Measure in the walnuts, all-purpose and millet flours, sugar, ginger, salt, baking powder, and yeast, placing the yeast in its own separate dispenser if your machine has one. The order in which these ingredients are placed in the pan should be reversed if the instructions for your bread machine specify that the dry ingredients are to be placed in the pan first, the liquids last. Bake on your machine's quick cycle.

To make the *biscotti*, cut the loaf when cool into slices approximately ¾ to 1 inch thick, then cut each slice into bars about 1 or 1¼ inches wide.

Place the bars on an ungreased cookie sheet and dry them for 10 to 15 minutes, turning them once halfway through the baking time, in an oven set to 350 degrees F. When they are lightly browned, remove them from the oven and transfer them to racks to cool.

For dipping the *biscotti*, if you're in a rush you can use one of the commercial chocolate dips, either brown or white, available in the baking section of most supermarkets. However, my own bias is very much toward making one's own chocolate dip. It really takes but a minute more, and the extra-rich chocolate flavor makes it well worthwhile.

DIPPING CHOCOLATE

4 one-ounce squares semisweet bak-
ing chocolate
½ cup heavy cream

contrasting chocolate for garnish, if
desired

Melt the chocolate in the top of a double boiler, stirring constantly to prevent the cocoa butter from separating out, and blend in the cream. Remove from the heat.

Dip the *biscotti* into the chocolate mixture until a third or a half of each is covered. Stand them on edge to dry on a cooling rack or prop them at an angle against the rim of a platter with no chocolate touching the platter.

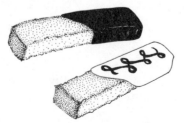

For an attractive finishing touch, once the dip has set on the *biscotti*, white chocolate can be drizzled over the dark, Jackson Pollock style. The first time I decided to try my hand at this bit of embellishment, I was temporarily stymied by the fact that, like most families, we have only one double boiler. I've tried to melt a small amount of chocolate in a regular pot. Let me tell you, it's tricky. Besides, one really needs only a couple of tablespoonfuls.

What I ended up doing was taking a small chunk of commercial white dipping chocolate and melting it in the microwave. Then with a toothpick I drizzled it in a crisscross pattern over the dark chocolate. The effect was fantastic.

Biscotti d'Anice

The Italian word *biscotti,* although now applied loosely to a broad range of cookies, means literally "twice cooked" and originally referred to those subtly and variously flavored rusks that so often accompany a hot drink or perhaps a glass of wine in their native country. Here's a recipe for the classic nut-crunchy version whose anise flavor, assuming you like that distinctive taste, goes so well with the milk-infused *caffellatte* served throughout Italy.

SMALL	LARGE
³/₄ cup milk, whole or skim	*1¹/₄ cups milk, whole or skim*
zest of 1 medium lemon	*zest of 2 medium lemons*
¹/₂ teaspoon vanilla extract	*1 teaspoon vanilla extract*
¹/₂ cup blanched almonds, toasted	*³/₄ cup blanched almonds, toasted*
2 cups unbleached all-purpose flour	*3 cups unbleached all-purpose flour*
¹/₄ cup sugar	*¹/₃ cup sugar*
2 tablespoons wheat germ	*¹/₄ cup wheat germ*
4 teaspoons aniseed, crushed	*2 tablespoons aniseed, crushed*
¹/₄ to 1 teaspoon salt, to taste	*¹/₂ to 1¹/₂ teaspoons salt, to taste*
1 teaspoon active dry yeast	*1¹/₂ teaspoons active dry yeast*

Pour the milk into your bread machine baking pan and add the lemon zest, vanilla extract, almonds, flour, sugar, wheat germ, aniseed, and salt. Place the yeast in its own dispenser if your machine has one; otherwise, scatter it over the rest of the ingredients in the pan. If it is to be placed in the bottom of the pan first thing instead, don't forget to reverse the order in which you add the liquid and the dry ingredients.

Bake the bread on your machine's quick cycle. Allow it to cool, then, for *biscotti,*, cut it into slices roughly ¾ to 1 inch thick and cut these slices into bars about 1 to 1¼ inches wide.

Oven-dry the bars on an ungreased cookie sheet at 350 degrees F., turning them once, until they are an even, toasty brown, which will take 10 to 15 minutes. Make sure they are completely cool before storing, and keep them in a tightly covered tin or jar.

Rye Rusks

Called *kryddskorpor,* or spiced rusks, in Swedish, these dried cookies have no spices in them. They are, however, flavored with orange zest, and back in the days of my youth, which my children place somewhere between the invention of the wheel and the ascent of Bill Haley and his Comets, oranges were considered a rare and exotic spice, at least in the north country where I grew up.

To harvest this spice for the rusks, peel the zest from the orange with a sharp knife. Wide strips, like those you'd have after peeling an apple, are fine here. Just try to minimize the amount of white pith you peel off with the outer, orange part, even though a bit of it in the bread will add a touch of pleasant bitterness to the rusks. You'll notice the use of gluten flour in this recipe. It's there to help the rather heavy rye dough rise.

SMALL	LARGE
¾ *cup milk, whole or skim*	1¼ *cups milk, whole or skim*
2 *tablespoons unsalted butter*	3 *tablespoons unsalted butter*
1 *tablespoon solid vegetable shortening*	2 *tablespoons solid vegetable shortening*
1 *tablespoon unsulfured molasses*	2 *tablespoons unsulfured molasses*
zest of ½ *medium orange*	*zest of 1 medium orange*
1½ *cups unbleached all-purpose flour*	2¼ *cups unbleached all-purpose flour*
¾ *cup rye flour*	1 *cup rye flour*
¼ *cup gluten flour*	⅓ *cup gluten flour*
¼ *cup sugar*	⅓ *cup sugar*
¼ *to 1 teaspoon salt, to taste*	½ *to 1½ teaspoons salt, to taste*
1½ *teaspoons active dry yeast*	2 *teaspoons active dry yeast*

Measure the milk into the baking pan of your bread machine and add the butter, shortening, molasses, orange zest, and the all-purpose, rye, and gluten flours, followed by the sugar, salt, and, last, unless otherwise directed in the instructions for your particular machine, the yeast. If your machine features a separate dispenser for leavening, spoon the yeast in there.

Use your machine's quick cycle to bake the loaf.

For the Rye Rusks, allow the loaf to cool, then cut it first into slices about ¾ to 1 inch thick and then into bars 1 to 1¼ inches wide. You don't need to be precise about the measurements.

Place the bars on an ungreased cookie sheet and oven-dry them at 350 degrees F. for 10 to 15 minutes or until they are a rich brown, turning them once halfway through the baking time for more even toasting. Cool the rusks thoroughly before storing.

In an airtight container, I'm told, rusks will keep for a very long time. I wouldn't know. Somehow my tin is empty within days, if not hours, of being stocked.

Zwieback

Not surprisingly, the originally German word *Zwieback*, long since anglicized, is yet another term that translates literally as "twice baked." Traditional to the northern European countries, zwieback has long been a favored accompaniment to compotes and preserved fruits. The zwieback's rather bland flavor is a perfect foil for the sweet syrup of the fruit, and its dry crispness complements the soft texture of the fruit itself. Although the combination may strike some as a rather plain dessert by today's voluptuous standards, it is a remarkably refreshing one on a warm summer's eve.

In the United States, zwieback has come to be associated nearly inseparably with infants. The rusks do make good teething biscuits, and the commercial varieties almost invariably portray a smiling baby on the box. The fact is, however, that zwieback and preserved fruits are one of those simple, forgotten pleasures deserving of universal revival.

In place of regular white flour, for a loaf destined for the zwieback tin I like to use the new white whole wheat flour developed at Kansas State University of Agriculture and Applied Science. Containing all the vitamins, minerals, and fiber of the whole wheat kernel minus the faintly bitter accent of so many dark whole wheat breads, it makes a "white bread" that, remarkably, is highly nutritious. The zwieback made from it is very light and open-textured.

If you don't have any white whole wheat flour in the house, simply substitute regular unbleached all-purpose flour and reduce the yeast in the recipe by ½ teaspoon.

SMALL	LARGE
¾ cup milk, whole or skim	*1 cup milk, whole or skim*
2 tablespoons solid vegetable shortening or lard	*3 tablespoons solid vegetable shortening or lard*
2 tablespoons unsulfured molasses	*3 tablespoons unsulfured molasses*

1 medium egg
2¼ cups white whole wheat flour
　(or unbleached all-purpose flour)
½ teaspoon ground nutmeg
¼ to 1 teaspoon salt, to taste
1½ teaspoons active dry yeast (if
　using all-purpose flour, reduce to
　1 teaspoon)

1 medium egg
3¼ cups white whole wheat flour
　(or unbleached all-purpose flour)
1 teaspoon ground nutmeg
½ to 1½ teaspoons salt, to taste
2 teaspoons active dry yeast (if us-
　ing all-purpose flour, reduce to
　1½ teaspoons)

Unless the instructions that came with your bread machine call for placing the yeast in the bottom of the pan, followed by the other dry ingredients and then the liquids, pour the milk into your baking pan and add the shortening or lard, molasses, egg, flour, nutmeg, salt, and yeast, reserving the leavening for its own dispenser if your machine has one.

Bake the bread on your machine's quick cycle.

To make Zwieback sticks, allow the loaf to cool, cut it into slices ¾ to 1 inch thick, then cut these slices into bars 1 to 1¼ inches wide.

Oven-dry the sticks on an ungreased cookie sheet at 350 degrees F., turning them once halfway through the baking time, until they are lightly toasted, which will take 10 to 15 minutes. Make sure they are completely cool before storing them in a tightly covered tin or jar.

Mandelbrot

In German the word *Mandel* means "almond," and *Brot* "bread." Yet I came across *Mandelbrot* in a village bakery outside of the German town of Oldenburg, not far from Denmark and the North Sea, that contained not a whit of almonds, but instead an abundance of hazelnuts. So what's in a name? These cookies are great, particularly when dipped in chocolate.

The dough is a sticky, heavy one. Check the inside of your bread machine baking pan 5 to 10 minutes into the first kneading cycle to make sure all the dough has been picked up by the mixing blade. If not, give it a little help by scraping down the sides of the pan with a rubber spatula.

Don't try to increase the ingredients to make a large loaf of this bread. The resulting dough would be more than the machine could deal with. Believe me, I know — I've tried it dozens of times.

SMALL

6 ounces frozen orange juice concentrate

2 tablespoons unsalted butter

2 tablespoons grated lemon zest

¾ cup chopped hazelnuts

2 cups unbleached all-purpose flour

⅓ cup semolina flour

¼ cup sugar

¼ teaspoon ground ginger

¼ teaspoon ground cinnamon

¼ to 1 teaspoon salt, to taste

2 teaspoons active dry yeast

Scoop the orange juice concentrate into your baking pan and add the butter, zest, hazelnuts, all-purpose and semolina flours, sugar, ginger, cinnamon, salt, and yeast, following the directions that came with your particular machine for incorporating the leavening, since some machines specify reversing the order in which the ingredients are placed in the pan and some models have a separate yeast dispenser.

Bake the loaf on your machine's quick cycle.

For *Mandelbrot* cookies, slice the cooled loaf into pieces about ¾ to 1 inch thick, then cut across the slices to make bars 1 to 1¼ inches wide.

Place the bars on an ungreased cookie sheet and oven-dry them at 350 degrees F. for 10 to 15 minutes or until lightly toasted, turning them once halfway through the baking time for even color. Cool them thoroughly on racks.

Dip some or all of them in chocolate if you'd like, following the instructions given with the recipes for Silver Birch *Biscotti* and Dipping Chocolate, pages 98–101.

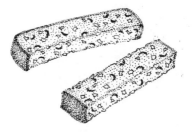

8 · Dessert Fondues

IN THESE RETRO-FIFTIES DAYS when Buddy Holly is alive and well and touring the country on countless car radios via classic rock stations and the King is taking his lickings courtesy of the U.S. Postal Service, my receipt of a fondue set as a Christmas present from our with-it teenager Tanya should have come as no surprise. But I had forgotten all about this culinary device, long since relegated to the musty corners of my memory, along with chafing dishes fashioned for tiny hot dogs and ring molds designed to imprint bold designs on green Jell-O suffused with canned fruit cocktail.

As it turned out, the fondue set was a great inducement to relaxed and rather cozy family dinners. Fondues are by nature a sociable yet informal event. Everyone seems to talk more around a fondue pot, particularly if its contents are sweet.

The original fondue was, of course, melted cheese. The long forks dipped into the communal pot held bite-size cubes of a homely bread, and a mellow wine cleared the palate between leisurely nibbles. Later, fondue bourguignonne made its appearance. The cheese gave way to oil and the bread was replaced by meat. Then finally, or so the story goes, sometime in the late fifties, a Swiss chef forgot a Toblerone bar beside the stove, and the chocolate melted. He dipped his finger in some, licked it off, and, voilà, the Toblerone fondue was born.

Chocolate and other dessert fondues provide an ideal use for leftover coffee breads, and particularly their crusts, if generous enough in their proportions. A fondue calls for a crusty bread anyway, to help give the fork something to hold on to when a cube of it is lifted from the dip. So when you trim a Banana Almond Loaf for petits fours or a Raspberry Cream one to be served à la mode, trim a little extravagantly so that what you are paring off isn't crust alone. Freeze these outer slices, and when you plan a fondue you'll have your bread on hand, needing only a brief defrosting period before it's ready to be cubed for serving. The bread will not be at its piping-hot-from-the-oven freshest, obviously. But that's all to the good. Truly fresh bread always has to be aged a little for a fondue.

One of the nice things about the home bread machine bakery is that, making your own loaves effortlessly and often, you can mix and match breads with fondues. Fruit breads go particularly well with chocolate fondues, for example, spice and nut loaves with butterscotch ones. Try cubes of Raspberry Cream and Pear loaves — pears and chocolate are made for each other — with a Toblerone Fondue, and serve squares of a Triple Chocolate Loaf with a mocha or mint dip. Dice the crusts of a Crunchy Caramel Apple-Granola Loaf or a Figs and Cream cake to accompany an Apple or a Hot Buttered Rum Fondue, and add some cubes made from the round slices left over in making a *Panettone Farcito*.

The palate can have too much of a good thing, of course. So when you serve a fondue, for a respite from these rich combinations do add to your bread board some squares from simpler loaves — Light Citrus, perhaps, or Sweet Peppermint Poppy Seed, Rose and Orange, or Peach Praline.

Toblerone Fondue

A chocolate fondue can be made from many kinds of chocolate — unsweetened, semisweet, sweet, chocolate chips — but there's something about those creamy Toblerone bars with their bits of nuts that makes a chocolate fondue special. So that's the chocolate I suggest here.

> *½ cup heavy cream*
> *12 ounces Toblerone chocolate*
> *½ teaspoon vanilla extract*
> *¼ teaspoon lemon extract or 1 ta-*
> *blespoon good brandy*

Warm the cream in a small saucepan, break the chocolate into pieces, and drop them into the cream, stirring over low heat until the chocolate is completely melted. Remove the pan from the heat and slowly, stirring gently, add the vanilla and lemon extracts, or the vanilla extract and brandy. Pour the sauce into a small fondue pot that you've warmed with hot tap water and place it over its warmer.

Your bread selection for a Toblerone Fondue might include some Light Citrus, Sour Cream Blueberry, Banana Almond, Kumquat Delight, Raspberry Cream, and Pear. For intense chocolate on chocolate, add cubes from a Triple Chocolate Loaf. On the side, set out a fruit platter with an attractive arrangement of fresh strawberries, grapes, and sliced kiwifruit garnished with sprigs of mint. In the wintertime, substitute a bowl of sun-dried apricots and pears. They'll all get dipped.

Mocha Fondue

Coffee and chocolate are a great combination. Blended into a fondue, they turn any homely dunking bread into an opulent dessert.

> ½ cup strong black coffee or
>   espresso
> 8 one-ounce squares semisweet bak-
>   ing chocolate
> ⅓ cup heavy cream
> 1 teaspoon coffee extract
> pinch of ground or freshly grated
>   nutmeg

Heat the coffee or espresso in a small saucepan over low heat and add the chocolate, stirring until the chocolate is melted. Blend in the cream, coffee extract, and nutmeg. Transfer the sauce to a fondue pot, warmed with hot tap water, and keep it quite hot over your fondue burner.

Probably by simple association, I think of squares of Coffee Nips Coffee Cake in connection with this fondue. But cubes from Rose and Orange, Double Almond, Chocolate Nut Delight, Cranberry-Orange, and Cherry Milk loaves are also excellent complements to a Mocha Fondue.

Super-Quick Chocolate-Mint Fondue

For an impromptu two-minute fondue that kids love after a cold day outside and adults aren't exactly impartial to either, take some of your frozen bread trimmings from the freezer and pop them into the microwave to defrost. Then turn your attention to this quick fondue sauce. Junior Mints are a fine choice for it. So are Peppermint Patties, After Eights, and other after-dinner mints.

12 ounces chocolate-covered mints
2 tablespoons unsalted butter
¼ cup heavy cream

For microwave preparation, place the mints in a microwave-safe bowl, add the butter and cream, and microwave for 2 to 3 minutes, until the mints are melted and the fondue is hot. Meanwhile, fill your fondue pot with hot tap water to preheat it. While the mints are melting, you can be cubing the bread. When you're ready to serve the fondue, empty the water from the fondue pot, shake off the excess moisture, and pour in the sauce.

For stovetop preparation, melt the butter in a small saucepan over very low heat, add the mints and stir until melted, then blend in the cream and stir until well warmed. Transfer to your preheated fondue pot.

Dish up cubes from a Banana Chocolate or a Peanut Butter–Chocolate Chip Loaf with this one if it's for the kids, and add some marshmallows to the bowl.

Mint-Chocolate Fondue

In our family, there can't be too much mint chocolate or too many chocolate mints. That goes for family fondue gatherings as well as other occasions. There's something special about the match between the cool mint flavor and the smooth sweetness of the chocolate that is quite compelling.

This fondue is even richer and mintier than the preceding one.

> *½ cup heavy cream*
> *8 one-ounce squares semisweet baking chocolate*
> *2 tablespoons peppermint liqueur or 1 tablespoon peppermint extract*
>
> *peppermint candy canes for garnish*

Pour the cream into a small saucepan, add the chocolate, and stir over low heat until the chocolate is melted and the mixture is hot. Remove from the heat to blend in the peppermint liqueur or extract. It might be a good idea to sample the mixture as you go. The dip may want a little less, or a little more, of the mint flavor than the recipe lists. Peppermint is a matter of taste.

Serve the fondue garnished at the last minute with bright bits of peppermint candy cane, and provide plenty of bite-size morsels from your last Cherries and Cheese and Yet Another Chocolate loaves. Toss a few fresh mint sprigs, if you have them, into the basket with the bread.

Super-Quick Butterscotch Fondue

There's something about a crisp fall or cold winter evening that seems to bring on the urge for something sweet and warm to nibble on. This fondue is for whipping up in next to no time when the craving for a rich caramel treat hits.

½ cup heavy cream
2 cups commercial butterscotch
sauce or ½ pound cream cara-
mels

Heat the cream in a small saucepan, blend in the butterscotch sauce or cream caramels, stir until smooth and hot, and serve in a fondue pot that has been preheated with hot tap water. Add some marshmallows, for the kids, and dates, for the grownups, to the bread basket. That's all there is to it, and the dipping is a delight.

Real Down-home Butterscotch Fondue

A butterscotch fondue, like a chocolate one, goes particularly well with nut and spice loaves, and one made from this easy recipe leaves any store-bought butterscotch out in the cold.

1 cup dark brown sugar
2 tablespoons unbleached all-
    purpose flour
⅛ teaspoon salt
1 cup evaporated milk
2 egg yolks, lightly beaten
2 tablespoons unsalted butter
¼ teaspoon vanilla extract

Stir the brown sugar, flour, and salt together in a heavy saucepan or in the top of a double boiler, then slowly blend in the evaporated milk. Place the pan or double boiler over low heat and, stirring constantly, add the beaten egg yolks and the butter. Cook the sauce, stirring often, until it is thick and creamy. Remove the pan from the heat and blend in the vanilla extract.

To serve, transfer the dip to a fondue pot that has been warmed with hot tap water and set it on its burner. Supply an assortment of Apple Wheat, Butterscotch Brickle, Peach Praline, and Crunchy Caramel Apple-Granola cubes. Small figs and apple wedges, fresh or dried, are marvelous dipped in this fondue as well.

Apple Fondue

Not all sweet fondues are based on chocolate or other confectionery sweets. Some fit right into the health-food, fruit-and-veggies, body-conscious mind-set of the eighties. A little wine (red, of course) is also healthful, according to the latest research, done where else but in France.

2 teaspoons unsalted butter
2 teaspoons unbleached all-purpose
    flour
1 cup good red table wine
2 tablespoons sugar
1/2 cup smooth applesauce
1/2 teaspoon ground cinnamon
zest of 1/2 medium lemon
1 cup apple juice
1/2 teaspoon cornstarch

cinnamon sticks for garnish

Melt the butter in a saucepan over low heat and stir in the flour to form a smooth paste. Let the roux brown slightly, then slowly add a little of the wine, stirring quickly to avoid lumping. As the mixture thins and becomes smooth, pour in the rest of the wine, add the sugar, and heat until the sugar is dissolved. Blend in the applesauce, cinnamon, and lemon zest. Blend a little of the apple juice with the cornstarch in a small bowl and stir to a paste. Add the rest of the juice to the sauce and heat well, but do not allow the mixture to boil. Stir in the dissolved cornstarch a little at a time until the fondue is thick enough to cling to a cube of bread dipped in it. You may not need to use all of the cornstarch solution. Pour the dip into a fondue pot that has been warmed with hot tap water and set the pot over its warmer.

Toss in a cinnamon stick or two to keep the aroma lingering above the fondue, and serve with cubes from *Pepparkaka, Panettone,* Pumpkin-Pie-Spice, Currant Ginger, and Figs and Cream loaves. Set out a small bowl of orange sections or quartered kumquats for both visual and gustatory sparkle.

Raspberry Fondue

A berry fondue is a wondrous thing. Need I say more? Our family favorite is probably a raspberry one. Another kind of berries can be substituted for the raspberries listed in this recipe.

> *1 ten-ounce package frozen raspber-*
> *ries*
> *½ cup heavy cream*
> *1 teaspoon lemon juice*

Let the berries defrost, then empty the package into a blender or a food processor and puree until smooth and fine. Pour the puree into a small heavy saucepan, add the cream, and stir constantly over low heat until the mixture is well heated and smooth.

Add the lemon juice at the last minute and serve the dip from your fondue pot, preheated with hot tap water, with any and all the chocolate bread cubes you can find, along with some from a Kumquat Delight, Sweet Peppermint Poppy Seed, Cranberry-Orange, Raspberry Cream, or Lemon Suzette Loaf.

Hot Buttered Rum Fondue

Sweet fondues are often flavored with brandy, wine, or a liqueur, as in the Mint-Chocolate and Apple Fondue recipes above. Here's one to serve on winter evenings when the snow is swirling silently around the house.

½ cup (1 stick) unsalted butter
1 cup firmly packed dark brown
  sugar
4 egg yolks
½ cup dark rum
few cloves

In a small heavy saucepan set over low heat, melt the butter and stir in the brown sugar, blending until the mixture is smooth. Once the sugar is dissolved, remove the pan from the heat and beat in the egg yolks one at a time. Return the pan to the heat and allow the mixture to thicken, stirring constantly. Just before serving, blend in the rum, toss in the cloves, and reheat the sauce briefly before transferring it to a fondue pot, prewarmed with hot tap water, set over its burner.

Checker a bread tray with cubes of a chocolate bread and a substantial white loaf, such as Light Citrus, to go with this fondue. *Panettone*, Currant Ginger, Peach Praline, Figs and Cream, and even Pudding Bread are also good choices here.

9 · Brown Betty, Crumb Crusts, and Bread Puddings

OUR PIONEER FOREFATHERS OR, for that matter, many of our parents would have found it strange that we actually buy ordinary leftovers for cooking these days. Croutons and bread crumbs found their niche in the culinary corner of the home as ways to use stale bread — not that there was that much of it. In those days every crust counted.

Well, the good news is that with a bread machine you won't have to buy commercial baked-goods leftovers anymore. You'll have plenty of your own. The even better news is that they make possible a variety of outstanding desserts.

Consider the simple bread crumb, for instance. Take some stale crusts trimmed from a loaf destined for petits fours, a layer cake, or some other sweet. Feed them through your blender or food processor until you have reasonably fine, evenly textured crumbs. These are crumbs the likes of which you can't buy. Chocolate, coconut, citrus — whatever the flavor of the bread used, it will accent the crumbs.

Slices of leftover bread for crumbs can simply be left to air-dry in an undisturbed corner of the kitchen. If needed in a hurry, they can also be toasted lightly in your toaster or, if they're too thick to fit in the slots, on an ungreased cookie sheet placed in a 350-degree F. oven for 10 to 15 minutes. Also, while a blender or food processor makes the quickest work of turning crusts into crumbs, the dry slices can be crushed between sheets of waxed paper or in a closed bag, graham cracker style.

Store your crumbs in an airtight container or freeze them for long-term safekeeping, and you'll be ready at a moment's notice to make, say, a homey brown Betty or a distinctive crumb-crust pie.

Apple Brown Betty

Vanilla Cream

When I was a child, I always wondered who this Betty was who could come up with such a yummy dessert. I was never quite sure which I liked more, the homemade vanilla sauce with which I would attempt to levitate and float the brown Betty in its dish or the brown Betty itself. In all probability it was the combination of the two, which is unbeatable.

Crumbs from a citrus or a spice bread are particularly suited to this quickly assembled dessert, the perfect warm and fragrant addition to an evening meal on a wintry day.

> *2 cups crumbs, crushed between sheets of waxed paper with a rolling pin or pulsed in a blender or food processor*
> *3/4 cup (1 1/2 sticks) unsalted butter*
> *3 cups diced peeled apples*
> *3/4 cup firmly packed dark brown sugar*

1 teaspoon grated lemon zest
1 teaspoon ground cinnamon
1/4 teaspoon ground nutmeg
1/4 teaspoon ground cloves
1/4 teaspoon salt
3 tablespoons lemon juice
3 tablespoons water

Melt ½ cup of the butter and mix it into the crumbs. Use a third of this crumb mixture to line the bottom of a generously buttered or oiled deep baking dish, preferably one that has its own lid.

Cover the layer of crumbs with 1½ cup of the apples.

Mix together the brown sugar, lemon zest, cinnamon, nutmeg, cloves, and salt. Sprinkle half of this mixture over the apples in the dish and dot them lightly with 1 tablespoon of the remaining butter. Then sprinkle them with 1 tablespoon of the lemon juice and 1 tablespoon of the water.

Lay down another third of the crumb mixture, followed by the other 1½ cups of apples. Scatter the remaining spiced sugar mixture over the apples, dot them with 1 more tablespoon of butter, and sprinkle over them the remaining 2 tablespoons of lemon juice and 2 tablespoons of water.

Cover the top apple layer with the last third of the crumbs and dot them with the remaining 2 tablespoons of butter. Put the lid on the baking dish and bake in a 350-degree F. oven for 40 minutes or until the apples are nearly soft when pricked with a toothpick or a fork.

Remove the lid from the dish and increase the oven heat to 400 degrees F. for 15 minutes or until the top of the brown Betty is nicely browned.

Serve the brown Betty hot with a ready-made vanilla sauce or, better yet, a pitcher of chilled homemade Vanilla Cream.

VANILLA CREAM

A vanilla sauce for a substantial pudding need not be terribly substantial itself. One doesn't want to overwhelm. The recipe given here is for a delicate, smooth, rich sauce. Those who like it sweet can add a couple more tablespoonfuls of sugar.

1¾ cups heavy cream
3 egg yolks
2 tablespoons sugar
2 teaspoons vanilla extract

Heat 1 cup of the cream in the top of a double boiler. Whisk the egg yolks and sugar together, then add them slowly to the hot cream and stir constantly over low heat until the mixture thickens.

Remove the pan from the heat, add the vanilla extract, and allow the sauce to cool, stirring occasionally.

When ready to serve the sauce, whip the remaining ¾ cup of cream and fold it into the custard mixture. Serve the Vanilla Cream in a pitcher from which it can be poured over individual helpings of the brown Betty. After all, someone may not be able to resist asking for seconds.

Basic Crumb Piecrust

The crumbs from the various loaves whose recipes appear in this volume make great quick piecrusts, needing only to be patted into place in a pie pan with a little melted butter before being filled. Certain pies such as custard and fruit mixtures benefit from having their shells chilled before filling, to keep them firm when the filling is scooped into them, and some benefit from a brief partial baking serving the same purpose. But in either of these cases, the piecrusts can easily be made in advance. Crumb crusts will keep in your freezer, in fact, for up to 3 months, and if you use the lightweight aluminum pie pans, they can be stacked inside each other, taking up reasonably little freezer space. With a premade shell and a quickly prepared filling, you can have a marvelous pie on the table in 15 minutes or less.

A chocolate crumb crust goes well with a creamy pie filling such as key lime or banana. A crust made with crumbs from a Lemon Suzette Loaf or from *Mandelbrot* is a lovely foil for sweetened fresh fruit like strawberries or sliced peaches. Covered with an only slightly extravagant layer of whipped cream and studded with chocolate curls or shaved chocolate, such a confection makes a sparkling and wondrously refreshing summer dessert.

The recipe given here is for a basic crust that derives its flavor primarily from the crumbs used to create it. If you are using crumbs from a strongly flavored loaf — such as chocolate, coconut, or peanut — or from one of the more highly spiced *biscotti*, omit the cinnamon and nutmeg listed in this recipe. The crumbs will give the crust enough flavor themselves.

> 6 tablespoons (¾ stick) unsalted
>   butter
> 1½ cups crumbs, crushed between
>   sheets of waxed paper with a roll-
>   ing pin or pulsed in a blender or
>   food processor
> ⅓ cup confectioners' sugar
> ½ teaspoon ground cinnamon (op-
>   tional)
> ½ teaspoon ground nutmeg (op-
>   tional)

Melt the butter in a small saucepan over low heat. Place the crumbs in a bowl and sprinkle over them the confectioners' sugar as well as the cinnamon and nutmeg if you are using those spices. Stir these ingredients together with a fork until you no longer see swirls of the white sugar. Pour in the melted butter and blend to a uniform pebbled consistency.

Reserve about ⅓ cup of the crumb mixture for a top sprinkling if desired and pat the rest evenly and firmly against the bottom and sides of the pie pan. For a perfectly even crust, take a second pie pan of the same size and press it into the first to firm the crumbs. Leave the pans together if you are freezing the crust, slipping the entire "sandwich" into a large freezer bag. If you reserved some crumbs for topping, slip them into a smaller bag and tuck them into the top pan for safekeeping.

To bake the crust, remove the top pan and place the crust in an oven set to 300 degrees F. for about 15 minutes. Let the piecrust cool before filling.

Deluxe Crumb Piecrust

Delicately flavored custard and cream pies, particularly, are enhanced by a rich piecrust. This one is enriched with nuts and a dash of cream. Save the trimmings from your more lightly flavored loaves such as Cherries and Cheese, Pear, and Rose and Orange, for this shell, so the nut taste comes through.

Almonds, walnuts, hazelnuts, and pecans are all fine nuts for a Deluxe Crumb Piecrust.

> *½ cup (1 stick) unsalted butter*
> *1¼ cups light-flavored crumbs, crushed between sheets of waxed paper with a rolling pin or pulsed in a blender or food processor*
> *⅓ cup grated nuts*
> *⅓ cup firmly packed dark brown sugar*
> *⅓ cup heavy cream*

Melt the butter in a small saucepan over low heat. Place the crumbs in a small bowl and, with a fork, mix in the nuts and brown sugar.

Drizzle the melted butter over the crumbs and blend it in, then do the same with the cream.

Press the crumb mixture evenly and firmly into a pie pan and flatten it with another pan of the same size.

Custard pies definitely want their shells prechilled or prebaked so as not to become soggy. Refrigerate the sandwiched crust to chill well or bake the shell in its bottom pan at 300 degrees F. for about 15 minutes. Allow a baked crust to cool before using it for a custard or cream filling. A shell intended for later use can be frozen still sandwiched between the 2 pans in a freezer bag.

Susan's Bread Pudding

Bread puddings are an endless source of dining delight, particularly during the winter months, when their hearty warmth lulls one into a pleasant postprandial drowsiness. There are myriad recipes for bread puddings, most of which fall into one of two categories: those calling for diced bread, and those in which the bread slices are left whole. Susan's Bread Pudding is of the first variety. It's scrumptious made with leftover crusts from a Sour Cream Blueberry, Rose and Orange, Luau, Butterscotch Brickle, Raspberry Cream, Crunchy Caramel Apple-Granola Loaf, or any chocolate loaf.

4 cups diced somewhat stale bread
3 cups milk, whole or skim
3 medium eggs
1/2 cup sugar
1 tablespoon lemon juice
1 teaspoon vanilla extract
1 teaspoon grated lemon zest
dash salt

Place the bread cubes in a large mixing bowl. Scald the milk in a saucepan and remove it from the heat. Separate the eggs, placing the whites in a small mixing bowl and the yolks in the milk, beating after each addition. Stir the sugar into the milk-and-egg mixture and add the lemon juice, vanilla extract, lemon zest, and salt. Continue stirring until the mixture is smooth and creamy. Pour it slowly over the bread and blend lightly with a fork.

Set the bread aside to soak in this mixture for about 5 minutes. Meanwhile, beat the egg whites until they stand in soft peaks. Fold them gently into the soaked bread.

Pour the pudding mixture into a well-buttered or oiled baking dish. Set the dish in a deep pan of hot water — the water should come at least halfway up the sides of the dish — in an oven preheated to 350 degrees F. Bake for about 40 minutes or until the pudding is bubbly and nicely browned.

Serve with a pitcher of cream and, if available, a scattering of fresh berries. They're heavenly with a bread pudding.

French Bread Pudding with Meringue

Bread puddings in which the bread slices are left whole, as opposed to being diced, are often called French bread puddings. Why I don't know. Perhaps it's because the whole slices are soaked like French toast. Or perhaps it's that French bread, used crust and all, makes a particularly attractive presentation of this variety. Of course, if you cover it all with a meringue, you don't see the pleasing array beneath.

Panettone, Sweet Peppermint Poppy Seed, Cranberry-Orange, Cherry Milk, Piña Colada, and, naturally, Yet Another Chocolate are all good loaves for this treat. From the subtle to the dominant, the

flavor of the bread used will give its own distinctive signature to the pudding. The variations are almost endless.

> *½ pound bread slices about ½ inch*
> *thick*
> *¼ cup unsalted butter*
> *4 medium eggs*
> *3 cups heavy cream*
> *⅓ cup sugar*
> *¼ cup maple syrup*
> *dash salt*
> *½ teaspoon cream of tartar*
> *½ cup confectioners' sugar*
> *½ teaspoon vanilla extract*

Spread the bread slices with the butter and lay them buttered side up in a lightly oiled 10-inch deep-dish pie pan or a round baking dish with sides at least 1½ inches high. Depending on how the slices have been cut, they may not all fit evenly into the dish. Just overlap them a bit if need be.

Separate the eggs, placing the whites in a small bowl to be set aside for the moment and breaking the yolks into a larger bowl. To the yolks add the cream, sugar, maple syrup, and salt. Beat well. Pour this mixture slowly over the bread slices and, with a fork, press the slices gently down into the mixture to make sure they all become soaked.

Bake the pudding in a 350-degree F. oven for about 40 minutes or until a toothpick inserted into its center comes out clean.

Beat the egg whites until frothy. Add the cream of tartar and con-

tinue beating until the whites form soft peaks. Beat in the confectioners' sugar and vanilla extract. Cover the bread pudding with the egg whites and bake for another 10 to 15 minutes or until the meringue is set and golden.

Serve with the satisfaction of having created a super homemade treat with your bread machine bakery.

Sources for Baking Ingredients

 MOST OF THE INGREDIENTS for the loaves in this book can be found on supermarket shelves or, failing that, in health-food stores. For the few rarer items needed, or for mail order for those who live somewhere in the boondocks and do much of their shopping by mail, the suppliers listed below are helpful sources.

Even if you don't need their products, you might consider sending away for their catalogs and pamphlets. In many of them you'll find sound culinary tips and tricks to use in your home bakery, not to mention an odd ingredient or two that might inspire you to create a quite new loaf.

Birkett Mills
P.O. Box 440
Penn Yan, NY 14527
Tel. (315) 536–3311

FREE PRICE LIST
NO CREDIT CARDS ACCEPTED

This mill specializes in stone-ground flours.

Brewster River Mills
Mill Street
Jeffersonville, VT 05464
Tel. (802) 644–2287

FREE BROCHURE

ACCEPTS MASTERCARD AND VISA CREDIT
CARDS

Organic flours and meals are available from this supplier.

G. B. Ratto and Co.
821 Washington Street
Oakland, CA 94607
Tel. (800) 325–3483

FREE CATALOG
ACCEPTS MASTERCARD AND VISA CREDIT CARDS

This firm carries a wide variety of flours and meals.

Jaffe Bros., Inc.
P.O. Box 636
Valley Center, CA 92082
Tel. (619) 749–1133

FREE CATALOG
ACCEPTS MASTERCARD AND VISA CREDIT CARDS

This firm features a large selection of organic grains, flours, and meals.

Kenyon Corn Meal Co.
Usquepaugh
West Kingston, RI 02892
Tel. (401) 783–4054

FREE PRICE LIST
ACCEPTS MASTERCARD AND VISA CREDIT CARDS

Various flours and mixes are available from this supplier.

King Arthur Flour
RR 2, Box 56
Norwich, VT 05055
Tel. (800) 827–6836

FREE CATALOG
ACCEPTS MASTERCARD AND VISA CREDIT CARDS

This firm carries all the basic flours along with some unusual ones, including white whole wheat flour. It also carries bulk yeast, flavor extracts, citrus oils, dried fruits, and just about anything else a baker could ask for.

Maid of Scandinavia
3244 Raleigh Avenue
Minneapolis, MN 55416
Tel. (800) 328–6722

FREE CATALOG
ACCEPTS MASTERCARD AND VISA CREDIT CARDS

Specializes in cake decorating and hardware but also carries flavors, extracts, and other ingredients.

Mister Spiceman
169–06 Crocheron Avenue
Auburndale, NY 11358
Tel. (718) 358–5020

CATALOG $1, REFUNDABLE WITH FIRST ORDER
ACCEPTS MASTERCARD AND VISA CREDIT CARDS

Spices and fruit extracts as well as caramel color are available from this source.

Tadco

900 Jefferson Road, Building 5
Rochester, NY 14623
Tel. (716) 292–0790
    (800) 724–8883

FREE CATALOG

ACCEPTS MASTERCARD, VISA, AMERICAN EXPRESS, AND DISCOVER CREDIT CARDS

Specializing in baking ingredients, this firm is a good source for flours, including gluten, pastry fillings, extracts, spices, barley malt syrup, and caramel color.

The Vermont Country Store

P.O. Box 3000
Manchester Center, VT 05255
Tel. (802) 362–2400

FREE CATALOG

ACCEPTS MASTERCARD AND VISA CREDIT CARDS

Stone-ground flours and cereals as well as other baking ingredients and supplies are available from this firm.

Walnut Acres

Penns Creek, PA 17862
Tel. (800) 433–3998

FREE CATALOG

ACCEPTS MASTERCARD AND VISA CREDIT CARDS

This company carries a broad range of flours, including millet.

Index